10 Minute Guide
to the Mac®

Stephen R. Poland

SAMS

A Division of Macmillan Computer Publishing
11711 North College, Carmel, Indiana 46032 USA

To Bob, Annis, Phil, Tom, Lenna, and Laura.

International Standard Book Number: 0-672-30063-x
Library of Congress Catalog Card Number: 91-62137

Acquisitions Editor: *Marie Butler-Knight*
Book Design: *Scott Cook*
Manuscript Editor: *Barry Childs-Helton*
Cover Design: *Tim Amrhein, Dan Armstrong*
Production: *Brad Chinn, Sandy Grieshop, Johnna VanHoose*
Indexer: *Sue VandeWalle*
Technical Editor: *Tracy Kaufman*

Printed in the United States of America.

Trademarks

Contents

Introduction

It's your first day at a new job, and your boss tells you to get cracking on a business proposal: "You'll use the Macintosh computer in your new office. It's easy to use, and you should have no trouble making the documents for the proposal." After your boss walks away, you realize you've never used a Macintosh before.

A few things are certain:

- You need a way to find your way around the Macintosh quickly and easily.

- You need to identify and learn the tasks necessary to accomplish your particular needs.

- You need some clear-cut, plain-English help to learn the basic features of the Macintosh.

Welcome to the *10 Minute Guide to the Mac.*

Because most people don't have the luxury of spending even a few hours learning a new computer system, the *10 Minute Guide* teaches the operations you need, in lessons that can be completed in 10 minutes or less. Not only does the 10-minute format offer information in bite-sized, easy-to-follow modules, it lets you start and stop as often as you like—because each lesson is a self-contained series of steps related to a particular task.

What is a 10 Minute Guide?

The *10 Minute Guide* is a new approach to learning about computers and software applications. Instead of trying to teach you everything about a particular computer or software package (and ending up with an 800-page book in the process), the *10 Minute Guide* teaches you only about the most often-used features and capabilities. Organized in lesson format, each *10 Minute Guide* contains between 20 and 30 short lessons.

You'll find only simple English used to explain the procedures in this book. With straightforward, easy-to-follow steps—and special artwork called *icons* to call your attention to important tips and definitions—the *10 Minute Guide* makes learning about computers and software quick, clear, and easy.

The following icons will help you find your way around in the *10 Minute Guide to the Mac:*

 Timesaver Tips offer shortcuts and hints for using the computer more effectively.

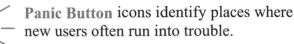 **Plain English** definitions clarify new terms.

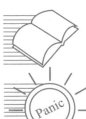 **Panic Button** icons identify places where new users often run into trouble.

 **System 7** icons identify features and operations that are enhanced by System 7, the latest version of Apple's operating system.

Additionally, a glossary of Mac terms is included at the end of the book, providing you with definitions and further clarifications, along with a list of popular software products for the Mac.

Specific conventions are used to help you find your way around the Macintosh as easily as possible:

Menu names	The names of menus, commands, buttons, and dialog boxes are shown with the first letter capitalized for easy recognition.
Numbered steps	Step-by-step instructions are highlighted, so you can easily find the procedures you need to perform basic Macintosh operations.
What you see on the screen	Within these numbered steps, the options you select from the Macintosh menus are printed in a second color and a characteristic font.
What you type	Within the numbered steps, the keys you press and the information you type appear in bold and in color.

The *10 Minute Guide to the Mac* is organized in 21 lessons, ranging from basic startup to more advanced file management and editing features. Remember, however, that nothing in this book is difficult. Most users want to start at the beginning of the book, with the lesson on starting the Macintosh, and progress (as time allows) through the lessons sequentially.

Who Should Use the 10 Minute Guide to the Mac?

The *10 Minute Guide to the Mac* is for anyone who:

- Needs to learn the Macintosh quickly.

- Doesn't have a lot of time to learn how to use a new computer.

- Feels overwhelmed by the seeming complexity of a new computer.

- Is reluctant to learn a new computer operating system.

- Wants to find out quickly whether the Macintosh will meet his or her computer needs.

- Wants a clear, concise guide to the most important features of the Macintosh.

What Is the Macintosh?

You could say that the Mac is a computer, made by Apple Computer, designed to be run with a *graphical user interface* made up of windows, icons, mice, and pointers—and that it has fantastic graphic and sound capabilities. You could go on to say that the Mac is consistent—almost all software for the Mac uses the same (or similar) command menus and operations.

More significantly, though, you should think of the Mac as a product-oriented computer; it helps you create an end *product* (such as a letter to the Editor, scientific diagram, or business proposal). Other computers give you the tools to create these products, but you often spend more time "learning the computer" than you do creating your product. The Macintosh stays out of your way and lets you produce.

Best of all—it should go without saying—the Mac is also fun to use.

Lessons

Macintosh Hardware Overview

In this lesson, you'll learn about the various Macintosh models, important purchasing considerations, how to set up their basic hardware, and how to turn them on.

Some Basic Mac Definitions

Whether you're a brand new Mac user, or are considering buying a new Mac, knowing the lingo will help you buy the Mac that suits your needs—and use it most effectively.

Hardware Components

The main component of a Mac is the *system unit,* a case that houses disk drives, circuit boards, and power supplies. One of the most important parts of the system unit is the *microprocessor,* or *CPU* (Central Processing Unit), which performs the calculations necessary for the computer to function. The Macintosh line of computers is built around the Motorola 68000 line of microprocessors.

Macs also have a *keyboard* and *mouse*, which are used to enter information. You learn more about these in Lesson 2.

Macs are either *compact* or *modular*. Compact Macs have a 9-inch monitor (screen) built into the case. Modular Macs have monitors that are separate from the computer itself.

Memory and Storage

RAM (Random-Access Memory) is the working area of the computer's memory. When you run a program or open a document, it's transferred from disk to RAM so you can work with it. The program or document remains in RAM until you save it back to the disk or turn the computer off. You can add more RAM to your Mac to improve its performance; each Mac model has, however, a maximum amount of RAM that can be added.

Macs can have two types of *disk drives*, used to store information. A *hard disk* is a mass storage device that holds a large amount of data. You'll use your hard drive to store software programs and document files. *Floppy disks* are small, removable versions of hard disks. They can hold only a fraction of the information that a hard drive can, and accessing your information on a floppy takes longer. You'll use floppy disks to install your application software, and to transfer data files between computers. (More about this in Lesson 10.) All Macs have at least one floppy drive.

Both RAM and disk storage are measured in terms of *kilobytes* (K) and *megabytes* (M). A kilobyte is approximately 1000 bytes, or characters, of information. A megabyte is about 1 million bytes of information. You can store about 200 pages of text in 1 megabyte.

Add-ons and Connections

You may want to connect other pieces of hardware to your Mac's *ports*, located on the back of the system unit. These are the outlets you use to connect additional hardware devices (such as printers and modems).

You may also want to add more hardware to the inside of your Mac. *Expansion slots* are the internal connecting points for additional circuit boards (such as network cards or MIDI devices) that perform specialized tasks.

Hardware Comparison

Now that you know the terms associated with the Macintosh line of computers, you can use the two tables below to compare the Macintosh models. Table 1-1 gives a comparison of the *low-end* (basic) models, and Table 1-2 compares the *high-end* (more powerful and more expensive) Mac models.

Table 1-1. Low-end Macintosh models compared.

	Mac Classic	Mac LC	Mac II si
Style	Compact	Modular	Modular
List Price	$999	$2499	$3769
Floppy Drive	One 3 1/2"	One 3 1/2"	One 3 1/2"
Hard Disk (optional)	40M	40M	40M
CPU	MC68000, 8 Mhz	MC68020, 16 Mhz	MC68030, 20 Mhz
Installed RAM	1M	2M	2M
Maximum RAM	4M	10M	17M

continues

3

Table 1-1. continued

	Mac Classic	Mac LC	Mac II si
Monitor	9-inch B&W	B&W or Color	B&W or Color
Speaker	Mono	Mono	Stereo
Audio Input	None	Mono	Mono
Expansion Slots	None	One	One

Table 1-2. High-end Macintosh models compared.

	Mac SE/30	Mac II ci	Mac II fx
Style	Compact	Modular	Modular
List Price	$4369	$6669	$9869
Floppy Drive	3 1/2"	3 1/2"	3 1/2"
Hard Disk (optional)	40M	80M	80M
CPU	MC68030, 16 Mhz	MC68030, 25 Mhz	MC68030, 40 Mhz
Installed RAM	1M	2M	4M
Maximum RAM	4M	10M	32M
Video Output	9-inch B&W	B&W or Color	Add-in card only
Audio Output	Stereo	Stereo	Stereo
Audio Input	None	None	None
Expansion Slots	1 Processor Direct (PDS)3	NuBus	1 PDS, 3 NuBus

Feature Considerations

When comparing Macintosh Hardware features, consider these points:

- Adding a MIDI (Musical Instrument Digital Interface) card or network card often requires a NuBus slot. Check with your Apple dealer for the specific requirements of your system.

- Desktop publishing and graphics applications use lots of RAM; their documents' files occupy a lot of disk drive space. These applications can be frustratingly slow if you don't have enough RAM and disk storage.

- In general, FASTER IS BETTER when it comes to microprocessor speed. However, if you use the Mac for simple word processing (and other nongraphic applications), even the slowest Mac model will suffice.

- The Mac II LC and II si support a built-in microphone, allowing voice/sound recording and playback.

- All Macs have a built-in network capability called AppleTalk. You do not need additional cards of interface circuits to connect your Mac to printers and other Macs. AppleTalk is somewhat slow; faster types of networks require you to add a circuit board to your Mac.

Plugging Things In

Connecting your Mac's components is a simple task. A few basic rules will see you through the setup process:

• Always turn off the Mac and other components before connecting or disconnecting cables.

• Cables and ports are labeled with matching *icons* (small pictures). Use the icons to help you plug things into the right place.

• All Mac connectors fit in their ports only one way. Rotate the connector (gently!) to find the right orientation.

• If it doesn't fit, don't force it.

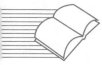 **Icon** An *icon* is a small picture, typically representing a real-world object. Macintosh cables and connectors are marked with icons to help the setup process.

To set up a Mac, follow these steps:

1. Plug the mouse into either of the ports on the keyboard (left side if you are left-handed, right side if you are right-handed). The ports are located at the top right and top left ends of the keyboard; they are labeled with an icon that matches the one on the keyboard cable.

2. Once the mouse is connected, plug either end of the keyboard cable into the other connector on the keyboard.

3. Insert the free end of the keyboard cable into the ADB port on the back of the Mac. The jack is located on the far left side, as you face the back of the Mac. (It's also labeled with a matching icon.)

4. Insert the power cord into its outlet on the back of the Mac, and into a grounded wall outlet. The Power On switch is located next to the power cord.

To help you get oriented, Figure 1-1 diagrams the back of a compact Mac setup. Figure 1-2 does the same for the back of a modular Mac setup.

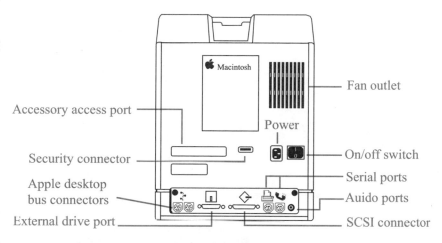

Figure 1-1. A view of the back of a compact Mac.

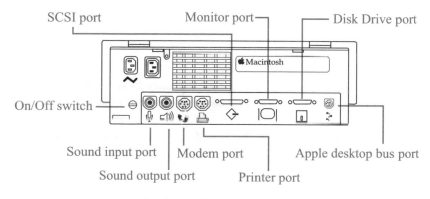

Figure 1-2. A view of a modular Mac's back.

Modular Macs come as a system made up of different components, so they require a few additional steps to complete the setup. You'll need to connect the monitor to the system unit.

1. Insert the monitor cable into the outlet on the back of the monitor. It's labeled with an icon that resembles a monitor. Tighten down the thumbscrews to secure the cable.

2. Insert the other end of the monitor cable into the monitor connector on the back of the Mac. (It's marked with a monitor icon.) Tighten down the thumbscrews to secure the cable.

3. Finish the setup by plugging in the monitor's power cord.

Having completed these simple connections, you are now ready to "power-on" your Mac.

Turning It On

The power switch for compact Macs is on the back left side of the case. Toggle the switch to 1 for on, and to 0 for off.

Modular Macs have both a switch on the back (it's round, located on the right side as you face the monitor) and a keyboard power-on key. The power-on key is marked with a small triangle, and is located in the top center or top right of the keyboard. Either the switch or key can be used to turn on the Mac, but a touch of the keyboard key is the most convenient, and recommended, method to use.

Turning On Your External Hard Drive If you have an external hard drive, be sure to turn it on first, and wait a few moments to let it get up to speed. *After* the external drive is on, you can turn on the Mac. The Mac will not start properly otherwise.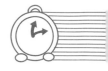

In this lesson, you have learned about the features and components of the Macintosh line, how to set up a Mac, and how to turn one on. All Macintosh models, once they're running, are "shut down" by software control. Lesson 2 will explain this simple procedure.

The Desktop

In this lesson, you'll learn about icons and the Macintosh Desktop, and how to use the mouse and Trash Can.

The Mac Work Area

When you turn it on, the Mac sounds a beep or chime, and displays a sequence of messages. A small picture of a smiling Mac (known as the "Happy Mac" icon) is displayed in the center of the screen, followed by a "Welcome to Macintosh" message. Finally, the Desktop appears.

The *Desktop* (or *Finder*, as it's technically known) is the working area for your computing activities. Much like the work surface of your real-life desk, the Desktop provides a place to work on documents, organize files and folders, and hold tools (such as a calculator, notepad, and ruler). All these real-world things have electronic equivalents; the Desktop is where you access them. Figure 2-1 shows a typical Mac Desktop.

The following items are always present on the Desktop:

- The *mouse pointer* (small arrow).

- A *disk icon*. Also known as the *startup volume*, this shows either as a floppy disk or a hard drive.

- The *Trash* icon, which shows as a trash can.

- The *menu bar* at top of the screen.

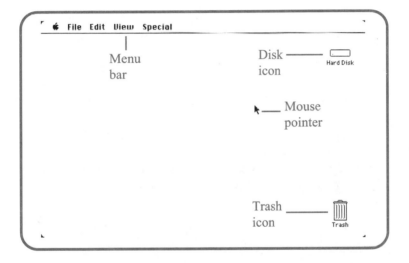

Figure 2-1. The Macintosh Desktop.

Using the Mouse

The *mouse* (the small device with the cable "tail") is your primary means of telling the Mac what to do. (You'll explore the details of the keyboard in a later lesson on typing and editing.) Use the single *mouse button* to trigger or sustain an action.

As you move the mouse around on your desk, the *mouse pointer* on the screen also moves in the same direction. Always hold the mouse with the cable pointing away from you. If you run out of room on your desk, pick up the mouse to reposition it. The mouse pointer will not move unless the mouse is touching the desk.

Here are some basic terms associated with the mouse, and what you do to perform the actions they refer to:

Point: Move the mouse pointer on the Desktop to a specific item on the Desktop, such as the Trash icon.

Click: Tap the button on the mouse once, quickly. Pointing to an icon and clicking will select the icon by highlighting it (for details, see the next section).

Double-click: Tap the mouse button twice in rapid succession. Double-clicking opens icons into *windows* (larger, more detailed screen views), or runs *applications* (programs which manipulate data).

Press and hold: Point to an object (usually a menu title) and hold down the mouse button, without moving the mouse.

Drag: Point to an object, and press the mouse button; while holding the button down, move the mouse. An outline of the object will follow the pointer, and when you release the mouse button, the object will leap to the pointer's new position.

Selecting Icons (Telling the Mac What to Do)

Selecting is how you tell the Mac which icon(s) or object(s) you want to be the target of action. Icons, file names, and lines of text can all be selected. Figure 2-2 shows the difference in appearance between a selected and unselected Trash icon.

Selected icon ——— Trash   Trash

Figure 2-2. Selected and unselected icons.

The selected icon shows on the left in the figure (only one Trash icon will actually be displayed on the screen). To select an object, follow these general steps:

1. Point at the icon with the mouse pointer, and click the mouse button. The icon will become *highlighted* (darkened for greater contrast, or shaded with color).

2. The next action you choose, such as copying or deleting, will immediately affect the selected object.

3. To deselect an object, just click on it again, or click on an empty part of the Desktop.

4. Remember: selecting one object always deselects any other selected object.

The Trash

The *Trash icon*, at the lower right corner of the Desktop, is a special icon used to discard objects (such as files, folders, or applications) you don't need any more. Putting an object in the Trash tells the Mac to prepare to delete the object from the folder or disk from which it came. (The Mac will not "empty" the Trash—that is, delete its contents—until you select **Empty Trash** under the Special menu.)

13

To put something in the Trash, use these steps:

1. Drag the unwanted object to the Trash icon. Be sure to position the mouse pointer on the Trash icon, so that the icon becomes highlighted.

2. When the Trash icon highlights, release the mouse button. The object will disappear and the Trash icon will puff up as if there were something in it (see Figure 2-3).

Trash

Figure 2-3. The "puffed" Trash icon.

Retrieving an Object From the Trash

If you mistakenly throw away an object, you can still retrieve it as long as the Trash icon is puffed up.

To open the Trash and retrieve an object:

1. Double-click on the Trash icon. It will zoom open into a window (see Figure 2-4).

2. The object will be somewhere in the window. Simply drag the object out of the Trash window to the Desktop.

3. Close the Trash window by clicking on the Close box in the upper left corner. The window will close, zooming back into the dimmed Trash icon.

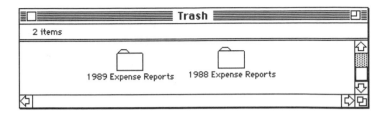

Figure 2-4. The Trash window.

Shutting Down the Mac

To end your Mac work session, you should shut down the Mac "gracefully"; the Mac needs to put away some behind-the-scenes files before it's ready to be shut down. To shut down a Mac, follow these steps:

1. From the Desktop, point to the Special menu title, then press and hold the mouse button. The menu will drop down.

2. While still holding the mouse button, drag the pointer down the menu until Shut down highlights. Release the mouse button. The Mac will put away some hidden files, and darken the screen. If you have a compact Mac, a final message will appear, telling you that it's safe to turn off the power switch, or Restart to resume your work session. If you have a modular Mac, the Shut down menu choice turns your Mac off completely.

In this lesson you learned about the Macintosh Desktop, icons, and how to use the mouse to move and open Desktop objects. In the next lesson you will learn how to use menus.

Lesson 3
Working with Menus

In this lesson, you'll learn to use the Finder's pull-down menus.

How Are Menus Used?

Macintosh menus organize and list commands and features available in the Desktop interface and in software applications. Because menus are used throughout the Mac, there are several key features to keep in mind:

- *Consistency:* The location of menus is, for the most part, consistent from one application to the next, as is the order of commands listed in the menus. You'll find the **Apple**, **File**, and **Edit** menus in almost all your applications, as well as on the Desktop. You won't have to learn different locations or operations for basic commands each time you buy a new application or utility.

- *Keyboard shortcuts:* Many menu commands offer a keyboard shortcut, so you don't have to use the mouse to select the command.

- *Dialog boxes:* Some menu commands have ellipses to their right (Print..., for example). This indicates you'll need to make choices from a dialog box that appears when you select the command.

- *Apple menu:* The Apple menu is a special menu which is available at all times. It lists the *desk accessories* (DAs) that are installed on your system. The Calculator, Notepad, Alarm Clock, and Scrapbook are a few examples of DAs available under the Apple menu. You will learn more about DAs in a later lesson.

Pulling Down a Menu

Macintosh menus are called *pull-down menus*. When you select the name of a menu from the menu bar at the top of the screen, the list of menu choices drops down from the menu bar.

To pull down a menu:

1. Point to the menu title at the top of the Desktop (File, for example).

2. Press and hold the mouse button. The menu will drop down. As long as you continue holding the mouse button, the menu will remain open. Releasing the mouse button closes the menu. Figure 3-1 shows the Apple menu pulled down.

Choosing a Menu Command

Once a menu is open, you'll need to choose the operation you want to perform. To do so, follow these steps:

17

1. Drag the pointer down the menu to the command you want. As you move the pointer down the menu list, commands will highlight. For example, open the File menu and select Open. See Figure 3-2 for a view of the File menu with the Open command highlighted.

2. When the menu item you want is highlighted, release the mouse button. The command will blink, the menu will close, and the command will take effect.

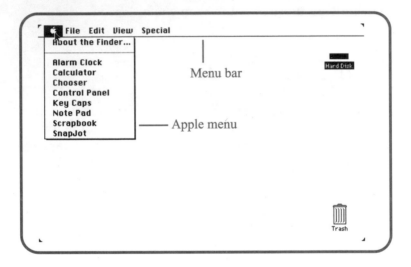

Figure 3-1. The Apple (⌘) menu.

In Figure 3-2, some menu commands are *dimmed* (or appear in gray). Dimmed options are not currently available. For example, a dimmed Cut option under the Edit Menu means that no text or graphic object is selected or highlighted. Because you have not told the Mac what to cut, that command is not available.

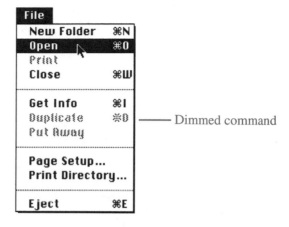

Figure 3-2. The File menu with the Open option selected.

Using Submenus

Some menus have *submenus,* indicated by small black triangles to the right of the menu commands. The submenus contain more detailed options for a particular command. Figure 3-3 shows a typical submenu.

To open a submenu, use the following steps:

1. Open the main menu, and drag the pointer to the command with the submenu.

2. When command highlights, the submenu will automatically open.

3. Drag the pointer to the right (over the small black triangle), and then onto the first submenu item.

4. Drag down the submenu until you reach the desired command, then release the mouse button. The command will flash, the submenu and main menu will close, and the command will take effect.

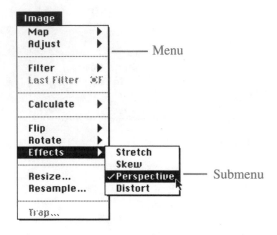

Figure 3-3. A submenu, shown opened.

Keyboard Shortcuts to Menu Commands

Many menu commands have keyboard shortcuts that allow you to choose a command without using the mouse. Shortcut key combinations appear to the right of the menu command. Look again at Figure 3-2 (the File menu) to see examples of shortcut key combinations.

The *Clover symbol* ⌘ and a letter are the most common shortcut characters.

To select a keyboard shortcut:

1. Select, highlight, or mark the object or text on which the command is to act.

2. Press and hold down the first key of the shortcut (in most cases, ⌘).

3. Press the second key (and the third, if necessary) of the shortcut. The title of the menu that contains the selected command will flash, and the command will take effect.

Table 3-1 lists some common keyboard shortcuts. You will learn more about the shortcut commands listed in later lessons.

Table 3-1. Common Keyboard Shortcuts.

Command:	Shortcut:
New Folder	⌘-N
Open	⌘-O
Print	⌘-P
Cut	⌘-X
Copy	⌘-C
Paste	⌘-V
Undo	⌘-Z

Menu Items with Ellipsis (...)

Many menu commands are listed with ellipsis (...) following the command name, indicating that more information is required for the menu option. When you select a command with an ellipsis, a dialog box will appear, prompting you for more information. (For more about dialog boxes, see Lesson 4.)

Check Marks in Pull-down Menus

Some pull-down menus show commands with a check mark to the left. The check mark indicates the current status of the menu selection. For example, Figure 3-4 shows the **Font** menu, with check marks next to the **14 Point** and **Palatino** entries. This means the current (default) font is 14-point Palatino.

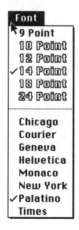

Figure 3-4. Menu items with check marks.

In this lesson, you learned the basics of Macintosh menus and keyboard shortcuts for selecting menu commands. In the next lesson, you'll learn how to respond to the prompts in a dialog box.

Lesson 4
Responding to Dialog Boxes

In this lesson, you'll learn how to work with dialog boxes.

Basic Components of Dialog Boxes

You use *dialog boxes* to provide additional information when it's required for an operation. Dialog boxes offer several ways to enter this information; these include text fields, radio buttons, check boxes, and pop-up menu lists. The Print dialog box, shown in Figure 4-1, provides an example.

| LaserWriter "Personal LaserWriter NT" | | | 5.2 | OK |

Figure 4-1. The Print dialog box.

Notice that the box asks you to enter the number of copies you want printed, which pages you want to print, and other relevant information.

Entering Information in Text Fields

Text fields are defined by rectangular boxes. When you position the arrow pointer in a text field, the pointer changes to an I-beam. Figure 4-2 shows the I-beam pointer in the text field used for selecting file names, in the Save As... dialog box.

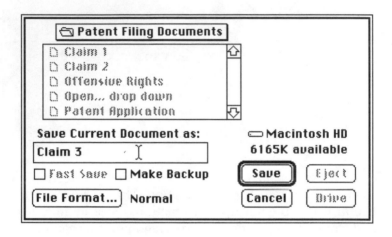

Figure 4-2. Dialog box, with the I-beam pointer in the **Save Current Document as:** text field.

Once you have the I-beam pointer placed, click the mouse button to place the *insertion point* (a flashing vertical line) in the field. You can now type and edit the field contents. You can also double-click in a field to select the entire field contents. Then the characters you type will replace the existing text.

Invalid Information If you enter invalid information in a field, an *alert box* will be displayed when you choose the **OK** button. Try a different value, or consult the software manual for valid entries.

24

Some text fields scroll horizontally to allow more characters to be entered. For example, the file name field in a Save As... dialog box shows only 25 characters of a file's name, but will scroll left to allow for longer file names to be entered.

Buttons and Check Boxes

Another way to indicate your choices in a dialog box is by using its buttons and check boxes; some are shown in Figure 4-3.

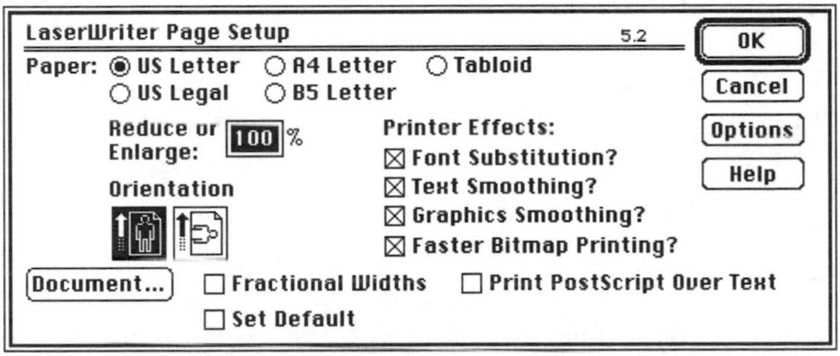

Figure 4-3. The Page Setup dialog box, showing buttons and check boxes.

Buttons are labeled with text, such as **Start Search** or **Don't Save**, describing the result of pressing the button. Pressing a button (clicking on it) carries out the action described on the button's label. (See the upper right corner of the figure.)

Check boxes can be either on or off. An **X** check in a box indicates the option is on; if the box is not checked, then it's off. Check boxes often appear in groups (like the **Printer Effects** check box group in Figure 4-3); when they do, you can check all options that apply.

Radio buttons (so called because they function like the buttons on an old car radio) always occur in groups. Only one can be on at a time. For example, you can only choose one paper size in the Page Setup dialog box (Figure 4-3). The US Letter button is selected in the figure. Selecting the Tabloid radio button by clicking on it will deselect US Letter at the same time.

OK and Cancel

The OK button is how you tell the computer that you've finished entering changes in the dialog box, and that you are ready to return to your document.

The Cancel button allows you to leave the dialog box and ignore any changes you may have made. Pressing the Esc key is a quick way to choose the Cancel button.

Quick Button Turn-on You can press the Return key to activate any button with a double border. The OK button is the most common button equipped with this shortcut.

Pop-up Menus

Pop-up menus allow you to choose from a list of similar options—fonts, for example. Pop-up menus are indicated by a small drop-shadow box, surrounding the current value. Sometimes a downward pointing arrow (as in Figure 4-4) also signals the presence of a pop-up menu.

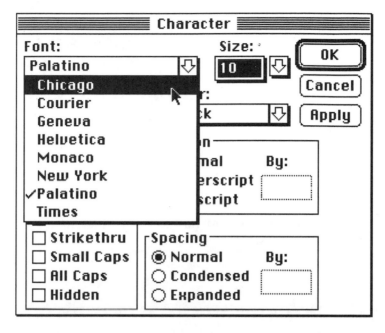

Figure 4-4. The Font selection pop-up menu in a character-formatting dialog box.

To change the value in a pop-up menu:

1. Point to the boxed option, and press and hold the mouse button. The list of available options will drop down. The current value will have a check mark to its left.

2. Drag the pointer down the menu; menu options will highlight in turn.

3. Stop at the option you want, and release the mouse button. The menu will retract, and the item you selected will appear in the shadowed box.

In this lesson, you learned how to enter information in dialog boxes. In the next lesson, you'll learn how to manage files and folders.

Working with Windows, Files, and Folders

In this lesson, you'll learn how to work with windows, files and folders.

Understanding the Macintosh's File System

In keeping with the Desktop metaphor, the Macintosh allows you to organize your files and applications in *folders* stored on hard or floppy disks.

Think of disks as filing cabinets, each of which stores many folders, which in turn store related *files* (such as those created for a certain client or project). Disks, folders, and files are represented on-screen by *icons* that reflect their function. For example, a folder icon looks like a manila folder, and the icon for a document file looks like a sheet of paper with the corner turned down. The Macintosh HD icon (in the top right corner of the Desktop) represents the hard disk of your computer. Figure 5-1 shows the Macintosh HD window, and several kinds of icons.

3-D Windows and Icons If your Mac is running System 7 (Apple's new operating system), your Desktop windows and icons will have a 3-D look.

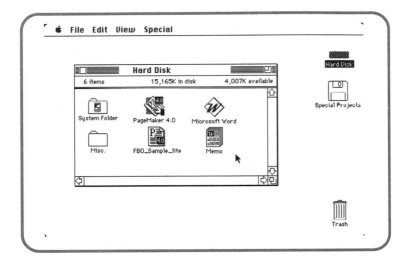

Figure 5-1. The Macintosh IID window, showing various icons.

Refer to this figure as you explore the following window features:

Disk icons represent either hard or floppy disks, and look like their physical world counterparts. Disk icons simulate the function of a filing cabinet. They hold your files, folders, documents, and other accessories.

Folder Icons resemble file folders. Folders help you organize and store your applications and documents in a logical manner.

Document icons represent documents and files (such as letters, memos, drawings) created with software applications. Document icons are often shaped like a piece of paper with one corner turned up, and sometimes resemble the icon of the application that created the document.

Application icons identify the software applications you use to create your work and carry out your computing tasks.

The following general operations apply to all folders, files, and disks:

- All file, folder, and disk icons can be easily moved around the Desktop by dragging them with the mouse.

- Folders can be "nested," (one inside another, inside another, etc.) several levels deep. The first folder you open is the *parent folder*. Folders within the parent folder are *child folders*.

- You can close a parent folder, without closing its child folder. When you later close the child folder, it will put itself away in its parent folder.

- You can eject a disk, even if its contents (folders, files, etc.) are left open on the Desktop. If you later close the folders, the Mac will ask you to insert the disk from which they came.

Opening a Disk or Folder into a Window

In order to see what's inside a folder or disk, you must open it into its window form. To open a disk or folder, you can:

1a. Double-click on its icon. The disk or folder will zoom open into a window. The name of the folder or disk is displayed at the top of the window.

or

1b. Select the icon with a click of the mouse button. The icon should become highlighted.

2. Drag down the File menu and choose Open. The folder or disk will zoom open into its window form.

Opening Shortcut You can press the ⌘-O key combination to open an icon once it is selected.

Window Controls

Every window has controls for editing your document. Figure 5-2 identifies these.

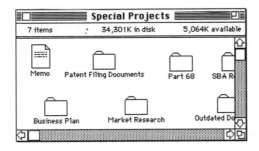

Figure 5-2. A typical window and its controls.

Refer to Figure 5-2 as you explore the following window features:

Title Bar: Displays the window's name (the same as that of the folder or disk icon you opened).

Close box: Click on the Close box to put the window back into its icon form. If the window is of a folder or disk, the window will zoom back into the grayed-out icon, and highlight the icon. If the window is of an application document (and the file has been saved), the window will close, leaving you in the application. To open any window you've closed in this way, just double-click on its icon.

Zoom box: Enlarges or shrinks a window with one click. Toggles the windows between two sizes: full-screen size, and the last size that was set with the Size box.

Scroll bars: Let you move the contents of a window so you can see more of it. You can scroll a window's contents by dragging the *scroll box*, clicking on one of the *scroll arrows*, or pressing and holding on a scroll arrow. (If everything is visible in the window, the scroll boxes do not appear, since there is nothing hidden from view.)

Size box: Allows you to change the size of the window. To do so, position the pointer on the Size box, press and hold the mouse button, and drag in any direction. The bottom right corner of the window resizes to follow the arrow pointer. Release the mouse button to complete the resize operation. (Note: You cannot make a window larger than the Mac screen.)

Creating and Naming New Folders

Once you open a window, you can create folders to store related files.

To create a new folder:

1. Click on the window in which you want to place the new folder; this makes it the *active window* (the one you're now working with). You can only create a new folder inside a disk or another folder.

2. Drag down the File menu and select New Folder, or press ⌘-N on the keyboard. The new folder (named Empty Folder) will appear, highlighted, in the active window. You can then change or edit the name of the folder.

To change the name of a folder:

1. Click on the folder icon. It can be either open or closed. The folder icon and folder name will highlight.

2. Type the new folder name. The old folder name will disappear, and the characters you type will center under the folder icon.

3. To finalize your change, point and click anywhere outside the highlighted filename area.

Accidental Name Change It's all too easy to accidentally select a folder or file and change its name. If you're careful, and catch the mistake before you do anything else, the Undo command under the Edit menu will restore the original file name.

Change Part of a Name If you have a long folder or file name, you can edit the part that needs to be changed by placing the insertion point in the folder or file name and inserting or deleting text.

In this lesson you learned about windows, files, and folders. In the next lesson, you will explore more windows activities.

Lesson 6
More Windows Operations

In this lesson, you'll learn how to move, layer, and change the view in your windows.

Moving Windows

Once you have a few windows open on the Desktop, you may need to move them to see their contents. To move a window on the Desktop:

1. Position the pointer anywhere on the window's Title Bar. Press and hold the mouse button.

2. Drag the window to its new location. As you drag, an outline of the window follows the pointer, and the original window stays put. When you release the mouse button, the window jumps to the new location.

Layering Windows

You can have several windows open at one time, so layering windows is an important operation. Open windows behave like sheets of paper stacked loosely on your desk. To work with a paper near the bottom of the stack, you must pull it out, and put it on the top of the stack. You manage Mac windows in the same way. The topmost window is called the *active window*, and is shown with several lines in the Title Bar of the window. Inactive windows do not have lines in the Title Bar. Figure 6-1 shows several layered windows, with the active window on top.

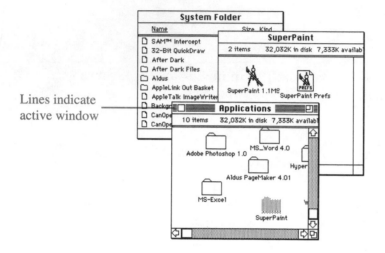

Figure 6-1. Layered windows. The active window is on top.

There are two ways to bring a window to the topmost layer of the Desktop (that is, make it the active window).

• If any portion of the window is showing, click on it, and the entire window will be brought to the front, overlying what was the topmost window.

• If you know there is an open window somewhere on the screen, but you can't see any part of it, find the open window's dimmed icon and double-click on it. The window will jump to the top layer of windows.

Changing File and Folder Display in a Window

The ʋieɯ menu provides you with several ways to view, sort, and organize files and folders. The ʋieɯ option applies only to the active window. Each window can have its own view setting. When you close a window, it remembers the last view setting. There are seven choices on the ʋieɯ menu:

Small icon	Displays icons at 1/4 normal size, and places their names on the right.
Icon	Icons are displayed at normal size. This is the most common (and default) window view.
Name	Displays file and folder names in an alphabetized list. The **Name** view also shows a file's size, kind, and date and time last modified.
Date	This view is similar to **Name** view, but sorts files and folders by date, listing the most recent first.
Size	Also similar to **Name** view, but sorts by a file's size. Unfortunately, folder sizes are not shown in this, or any view.
Kind	Files and folders are listed, alphabetized by file kind (application, document, folder, system file, etc.)
Color	If you have a color Macintosh, the **Color** option sorts files and folders by color. You choose the color of an icon by selecting it, then picking a color under the **Color** menu.

37

To illustrate the differences, Figure 6-2 shows three windows viewed by **Name**, **Icon**, and **Small Icon**.

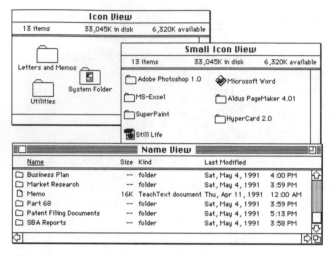

Figure 6-2. Windows viewed by **Icon**, **Small Icon**, and **Name**.

To change the view of a window, follow these steps:

1. Make the window active by clicking on it (or on its dimmed icon).

2. Drag down the **View** menu and select one of the **View** options.

In this lesson you learned how to move, layer, and alter the view in your windows. In the next lesson you'll explore Mac dialog boxes.

Lesson 7
Typing, Editing, Cutting, and Pasting

In this lesson, you'll learn the basics of typing and editing on the Mac.

The Basics of Typing and Editing

Whether you are typing in a word processor, changing a file name, or adding text labels to a graphics diagram, how you type and edit is the same across all Mac operations and applications. There are a few rules to keep in mind as you explore typing and editing on the Mac:

- You know you're in typing mode when the mouse pointer changes to an *I-beam pointer* (pronounced "eye-beam"). If it's not present, you can't begin typing. Figure 7-1 shows the I-beam pointer.

$$\text{I}$$

Figure 7-1. The I-beam pointer.

- When typing in a word processor, type complete paragraphs before hitting the Return key. The Mac will take care of moving words to the next line without splitting them. This feature is called *word wrap*.

• Once you have *selected* (highlighted) a section of text, you can delete it, move it, or change the way it looks.

• Unless you've selected text, the Mac is always in insert mode. As you type or delete new characters, any existing characters move right or left to accommodate your changes.

Placing the Insertion Point and Typing

When you move the mouse pointer over a file name, into a text field, or into the work area of a word processor, the pointer changes to an I-beam.

The I-beam pointer controls the location of the *insertion point* (a flashing vertical bar). Click the mouse button to place the flashing insertion point at the location of the pointer. Figure 7-2 shows a line of text, the insertion point, and the I-beam pointer.

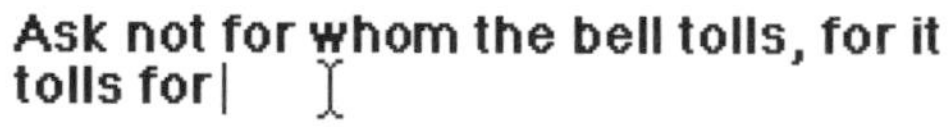

Ask not for whom the bell tolls, for it tolls for| I

Figure 7-2. The insertion point and I-beam pointer.

As you type, letters appear to the left of the insertion point as it moves right. If you set the insertion point in the middle of a word or line, the characters to the right of the insertion point will be pushed out to the right to make room for the new characters.

You can use either the mouse or the **Arrow** keys on the keyboard to change the insertion point's location. Moving the I-beam pointer does not change the location of the insertion point until you click the mouse button.

Each time you press the **Delete** key on the keyboard, a character to the left of the insertion point is deleted. Any text to the right of the insertion point will flow left to fill the space left by the characters you delete.

Using the Mouse to Select Text

You can select text in the same way, and for the same reasons, that you select icons. Selecting text blocks makes it easy to delete, move, or copy whole sections of text at one time.

To select a block of text, use the following steps:

1. Place the I-beam pointer to the left of the first character of text you want to select.

2. Press and hold the mouse button while dragging the I-beam cursor to the right over the text. The text will be highlighted a character at a time, showing you exactly what you have selected. You can also drag the mouse up or down to select an entire line (or more) of text at a time.

   Selecting a Word To quickly select an entire word, place the I-beam anywhere over the word and double-click the mouse button.

You can deselect text any time by clicking the mouse button anywhere in the document. Figure 7-3 shows some examples of selected text.

41

This line has one **word** selected.

This section of **text has several words** selected.

Figure 7-3. Example of selected text.

Replacing Text To replace a section of text quickly, highlight it, then type the new text. The highlighted block will be completely replaced by the characters you type.

Using the Keyboard to Select Text

You can also use the keyboard to move the insertion point and to select sections of text. The **Up, Down, Right,** and **Left Arrow** keys (on the right-hand side of the keyboard) move the insertion point. The **Up** and **Down Arrow** keys move the insertion point to the line above or below. The **Right** and **Left Arrow** keys move the insertion point one character left or right.

To select a section of text using the **Arrow** keys, follow these steps:

1. Position the insertion point with the I-beam pointer or **Arrow** keys.

2. Press and hold the **Shift** key.

3. Press either the **Right** or **Left Arrow** keys to select a character at time. To select a word at a time, hold the **Option** and **Shift** keys while arrowing over the text to be highlighted.

Cutting and Pasting with the Clipboard

The *Clipboard* is a holding area for whatever (either text or graphic pictures) you cut or copy from a document. Choosing **Cut** from the **Edit** menu removes the selected text or graphic from the document, and puts it on the Clipboard. Choosing **Copy** copies the selected text or graphic to the Clipboard, leaving the original selection in place.

Once you *cut* or *copy* an object to the Clipboard, it will remain there until you replace it (by cutting or copying a new object), or until you shut down the computer. Changing or leaving an application does not affect the contents of the Clipboard; therefore, you can move graphics and text between applications using the Clipboard.

You can *paste* an object from the Clipboard into a new area of your current document—or you can switch applications, and paste it into an entirely different document. Pasting inserts a copy of what's on the Clipboard at the location of the insertion point, leaving the contents of the Clipboard intact.

Follow these steps to cut (or copy) and paste:

1. Using the mouse or keyboard, select the object or block of text.

2. Drag down the **Edit** menu and select **Cut** or **Copy**, depending on your intent.

3. If you want to paste the contents of the Clipboard in a new location, set the insertion point at the new location. Drag down the **Edit** menu and choose **Paste**. The text block or graphic object will be inserted at the insertion point.

Keyboard Shortcuts for Cut, Copy, and Paste
Use ⌘-X to Cut, ⌘-C to Copy, and ⌘-V to Paste.

The Clipboard can hold only one item at a time, and is normally not visible (some applications allow you to show the Clipboard). Remember, cutting and copying overwrites whatever is on the Clipboard. If you need to save multiple text blocks or graphic objects, paste the contents of the Clipboard into the Scrapbook each time you cut or copy. You will learn more about the Scrapbook in the lesson on Desk Accessories.

Undo It Don't forget the **Undo** command under the **Edit** menu. If you mistakenly clear a section of text, drag down the **Edit** menu and choose **Undo**, or press ⌘-Z. The deleted text will reappear in its original location.

In this lesson you learned about the typing and editing features that are used in all Mac operations and applications. In the next lesson you'll learn about enhancing text with fonts.

Lesson 8
Understanding
Fonts

In this lesson, you'll learn about fonts and printing considerations.

Fonts, Serifs, and Sizes

A *font* is set of characters created with a consistent design. All the characters in the font share certain attributes such as thickness of lines or degree of curves. Figure 8-1 shows several different fonts.

Times	ABCDEFGabcdefg
Courier	ABCDEFGabcdefg
Helvetica	ABCDEFGabcdefg
Garamond	ABCDEFGabcdefg
Zapf Ellipt	ABCDEFGabcdefg

Figure 8-1. Several Macintosh fonts.

Fonts are usually categorized as *serif* or *sans serif*. Serifs are the "feet" added to the main strokes of a letter.

45

If a font does not have serifs, it's called a sans serif (without serifs) font. Figure 8-2 shows serif and sans serif fonts.

Times is a *serif* font.
Helvetica is a *sans serif* font.

Figure 8-2. Serif and sans serif fonts.

The characters of a font can appear in many different *character sizes*; these are measured in *points*. There are 72 points in one inch, so a 72-point font is about 1 inch tall. Figure 8-3 shows several point sizes of the Helvetica font.

10 point

12 point

14 point

18 point

24 point

Figure 8-3. Five point sizes of Palatino.

Screen Fonts vs Printer Fonts

The Mac comes with two sets of fonts. They can be divided into two categories: *laser printer fonts* and *screen fonts*. Table 8-1 lists the standard Mac fonts in these two categories.

Table 8-1. The standard Mac fonts.

Laser Printer Fonts:	Screen Fonts:
Times	New York
Helvetica	Geneva
Courier	Monaco
Symbol	Chicago
	Venice

The *laser printer fonts* are designed to be printed on high-resolution printers such as laser printers. (The Apple LaserWriter is an example.)

The characters you see on your Mac screen, which appear in the typefaces called *screen fonts*, are made up of tiny dots. 72 of these dots make up one inch. This measure (dots per inch, or *DPI*) is known as the *resolution* of your screen—in this case, 72 dots per inch. By comparison, a laser printer puts the dots on the page at a resolution 300 dots per inch. The more dots per inch, the sharper the characters and images look.

> **Resolution** The measure of sharpness of text and graphics (as displayed on your screen or printed by printing devices). The higher the *resolution*, the sharper the text image will be. The Mac screen has a resolution of 72 dots per inch. A LaserWriter Printer has a resolution of 300 dots per inch.

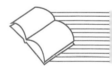

The screen fonts are designed to be printed on low-resolution devices, such as the Mac screen and the Apple ImageWriter printer.

Using Fonts In Your Documents

Most Mac applications offer two menus that give you control over the appearance of text: the Font menu and the Style (sometimes called Format) menu.

The Font menu is similar in all Macintosh applications; it typically lists the size of the font first, and the actual font name second. Figure 8-4 shows a typical Font menu.

The check mark next to 12 Point and Chicago indicates that the current (default) font choice is 12-point Chicago. When you start typing, the characters will appear in that font.

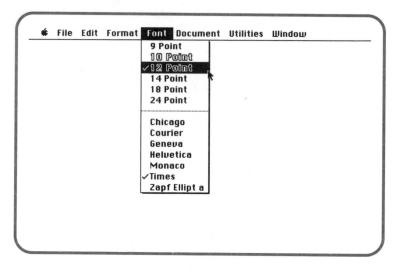

Figure 8-4. A typical Font menu.

Choosing a Font and Type Size

You can choose a font before you start typing, or type in the existing (default) font and change it later. To select a font and type size, follow these steps:

1. Place the insertion point where you want to start typing, or select the text you want to change.

2. Drag down the Font menu and select a size. The selected section of text will change to the size you selected. If you just placed the insertion point, you will see no change until you start to type.

3. Drag down the Font menu and choose a font name. The selected section of text will change to the font you picked. Again, if you just placed the insertion point, no changes will be seen until you type.

Changing the Style of Your Text

Style refers to a special treatment of the characters in a font. **Bold**, *Italic*, <u>Underline</u>, and Shadow are all style choices you can apply to the characters you type. Figure 8-5 shows several styles available on the Mac.

Bold

Italic

Bold Italic

<u>Underline</u>

Outline

Shadow

Figure 8-5. Mac style choices.

As you can see from Figure 8-5, characters in the same font and size can have more than one style—and each style in the figure shows itself with its correct name.

Applying a Style

You apply a type style to text the same way you change a font or type size. Follow these steps to apply a style to a section of text:

1. Select the section of text you want to change.

2. Drag down the style menu (or Format menu, depending on your application). Choose the style you want. When you release the mouse button, the text you selected will change to the style you picked.

In this lesson, you learned about the various aspects of Mac fonts. In the next lesson, you'll learn about managing files and folders.

Lesson 9
Managing Files and Folders

In this lesson, you'll learn how to organize, copy, and name files and folders.

Moving versus Copying

Moving and copying might look like the same operation—since both involve dragging an icon of a file or folder from one location to another—but they are not the same. *Copying* only takes place when you drag an icon from one *disk* to another *disk*. The copy process makes a duplicate file, and copies it to the new location, leaving the original file in place.

For example, if you drag a file from a floppy disk window to a folder or window on the hard disk, the file will be copied from the floppy to the hard disk. The original is left on the floppy. On the other hand, if you drag a file from one folder to another on the same hard drive, you'll *move* the file; it will no longer occupy its original location.

Quick Copy If you want to *copy* a file from one window to another, hold down the **Option** key while you drag the icon to its new location. The original icon will remain where it was, and a copy will be placed in the new location.

Moving a File or Folder

Figure 9-1 shows a file being moved from one window to another. You will use this procedure often when organizing your files.

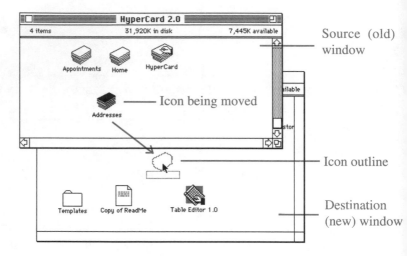

Figure 9-1. A document file being moved from one window to another.

Follow these steps to move files and folders.

1. Arrange the windows on the Desktop so that the file to be moved—and some portion of the destination disk, folder, or window—is showing.

2. Drag the object from its current location to the new location, making sure that the arrow pointer is inside the destination object. (Remember: as you drag the icon, an outline of the icon follows the mouse pointer.) Disks and folders will highlight when you are on target with the pointer; if the destination icon does not highlight,

you're not quite on target. Windows do not give any indication of when the pointer is on target, but with a little practice, you will easily move objects from window to window.

Copying a File or Folder

Remember that copying takes place between two disks. Follow the steps below to copy a file or folder from a floppy disk to your hard drive:

1. Insert the floppy disk into the opening on the front of the Mac. The label should face up, and the metal shutter goes in first. The floppy disk icon will appear on the Desktop below the hard drive icon.

2. Double-click on the floppy disk icon to open it, and do the same for the hard disk icon if it's not already open.

3. Choose an icon of a file or folder on the hard drive, and drag it to the floppy disk window. When you release the mouse button, the Copy *status box* (showing the progress of the copy) will appear at the top of the screen. Figure 9-2 shows this status box.

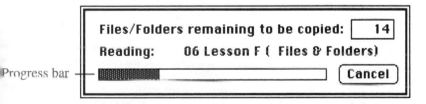

Progress bar

Figure 9-2. The Copy status box.

4. When the copying is complete, the icon will appear in the floppy disk window, and the original remains in the hard drive window.

Moving a Group of Files

You can move several files at a time by selecting them as group. Follow these steps to select and move a group of files.

1. Point, press, and drag over the group of icons; make sure the pointer does not touch any one of the folders. The icons become highlighted (to show their participation in the grouping) as the pointer and the rectangular selection area pass over them. Figure 9-3 shows the grouping process in action.

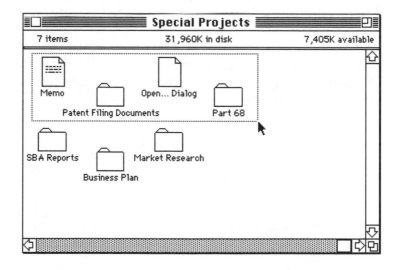

Figure 9-3. Selecting a group of icons with the mouse.

2. Release the mouse button once you have selected the group of files you want to move.

3. Point to any one of the highlighted files, then press and hold the mouse button. You can now drag the group to a new location. Only the tip of the pointer needs to be in the new folder, window, or disk. As you drag, as usual, an outline of the selected icons will follow the pointer. Figure 9-4 shows the drag in progress.

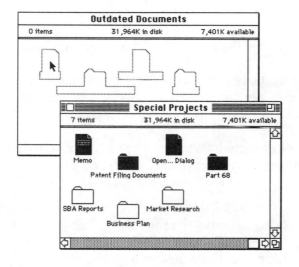

Figure 9-4. Dragging a group of icons to a new location.

4. When you release the mouse button, the files will disappear from their original location, and reappear in the new folder.

Naming Files, Folders and Disks

From time to time you will want to rename your folders and documents. You can follow the steps below whether your files are viewed by icon, or in one of the list formats. You can also rename disks with these steps.

Remember, a file or folder name can be as long as 32 characters, and a disk name can be 27 characters long. So be as descriptive as possible when naming files, folders, and disks.

To change the name of a folder, file, or disk:

1. Select the object's icon. Click on the icon's name. The mouse pointer will change to an I-beam, and the file name will highlight.

2. Type the new icon name. The old name will disappear, and the characters you type will center under the icon.

 Changing File Names in System 7 In addition to highlighting the file name when you click on it, System 7 draws a rectangular box around the file name. Once the box appears, you can retype or edit the file name.

Duplicating a File

If you want to create an exact copy of a file or folder, you can use the **Duplicate** option under the **File** menu. To create a duplicate of a file or folder, try these steps:

1. Select the file or folder to be duplicated.

2. Drag down the File menu and choose Duplicate, or press ⌘-D on the keyboard. A status box will appear at the top of the screen, showing the duplication's progress. When the process is complete, the duplicate icon will appear next to the original. The Mac will append the words Copy of to the original icon name (e.g., Copy of System Folder). You can rename the new icon as usual.

In this lesson, you learned how to create, move, copy, and name files and folders. In the next lesson, you'll learn how to format and manage floppy disks.

Lesson 10
Managing Disks and Disk Drives

In this lesson, you'll learn about Macintosh disks and disk drives.

Floppy Disks

Floppy disks provide a way to distribute software, move files from one computer to another, and back up hard disk drives.

All Macs have at least one *floppy disk drive*, located on the front of the system unit. You insert a 3 1/2-inch *floppy disk* into the drive to be read by the computer. Figure 10-1 shows what a floppy disk looks like.

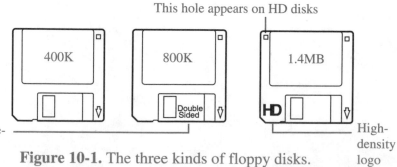

This hole appears on HD disks

Double-sided label

High-density logo

Figure 10-1. The three kinds of floppy disks.

The maximum amount of information a 3 1/2-inch floppy disk can store varies widely. The following list gives the names and capacities of Macintosh floppy disks.

- *Single-sided* (400K, labeled "Single Sided"). Information is stored on one side of the disk. (Note: these floppy disks are not very common any more, but you may encounter them.)

- *Double-sided* (800K, labeled "Double Sided"). Information is stored on both sides of the disk.

- *High-density* (1.4 megabytes, labeled "HD"). Information is stored on both sides of these disks in a compressed format.

High-density disks can be used only in *FDHD* (floppy disk, high-density) drives. All new Macintoshes (including the Classic, II LC, and II si) are equipped with this drive, also known as a SuperDrive. The SuperDrive can read and write to both Macintosh disks and to MS-DOS formatted disks.

Inserting and Ejecting Floppy Disks

There is one way to insert a floppy disk, and two ways to eject it.

To insert a disk:

1. Hold the disk with label facing up, and insert it (metal shutter first) into the slot in the front of the Mac.

2. The drive will spin and an icon of the disk will appear on the Mac Desktop, or a dialog box will appear if the disk is not *initialized* (see the next section for details).

To eject a disk (two methods):

1. Select the disk on the Desktop, drag down the File menu and select Eject, or press ⌘-E to eject the disk. A dimmed image of the disk's icon will remain on the Desktop. As you will see later in this lesson, you'll need the dimmed icon when copying disks. Figure 10-2 shows the dimmed image of a floppy disk.

Letters & Memos

Figure 10-2. The dimmed icon of a floppy disk.

2. Drag the disk icon to the Trash, the disk will eject and its icon will disappear.

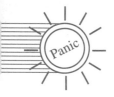

Stuck Disk Occasionally a disk may be physically damaged, so it won't eject automatically. To eject the disk manually, gently insert a straightened paper clip into the small hole at the right of the disk drive. This will mechanically trigger the eject mechanism of the drive and force the disk out.

Initializing Floppy Disks

Before your computer can put information on a disk, the disk needs some basic information about your computer and disk drive. Placing this information on a disk is called *initializing* or *formatting*.

To initialize a blank disk, follow these steps:

1. Insert the blank disk in the disk drive. A dialog box (Figure 10-3) will appear, telling you that the disk is unreadable, and asking whether you want to initialize it.

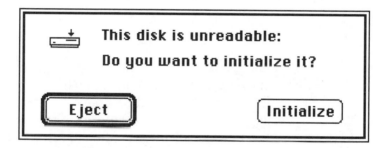

Figure 10-3. The disk initialization dialog box for 1.4M floppy disks.

2. If the floppy you inserted was a 400K or 800K, the dialog box will show three buttons; these allow you to eject the disk, initialize it one-sided, or initialize it two-sided. If the disk you inserted is 400K, click on One-sided. For 800K disks, choose Two-sided. If the disk is an 1.4M, the dialog box shows only two buttons; Eject and Initialize. Click on the Initialize button.

3. The next dialog box warns that you are about to erase any existing information on the disk (see Figure 10-4). Click on the Erase button to continue the initialization process.

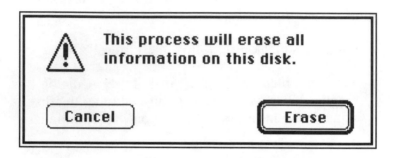

Figure 10-4. The Erase warning dialog box.

4. The Name dialog box, the final one in this process (Figure 10-5), now appears—prompting you for a name for the disk. Type a name containing up to 27 characters, leaving out colons (:). All other characters are allowed in disk names. Click the OK button to finish the process.

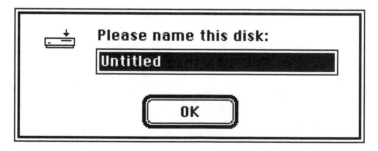

Figure 10-5. The Name dialog box.

As the disk initializes, you will see three messages in a status box: Formatting Disk..., Verifying Format..., and Creating Directory.... When the status box disappears, initialization is complete.

Disk Recognition The FDHD drive (SuperDrive) does not recognize high-density disks initialized in a 400K or 800K disk drive. It will respond by asking if you want to initialize the disk. DO NOT initialize the disk. Eject it, back up the data to the hard drive, and place the data on a high-density disk which has been formatted in a SuperDrive.

Locking and Unlocking Floppy Disks

You can lock a diskette, and thus prevent information on the disk from being changed or erased. To lock a disk:

1. Hold the disk with its label side away and its metal shutter pointing down.

2. There is a colored tab in the upper right corner. Slide the tab toward the outer edge of the disk. This will leave a opening where the tab was.

3. To unlock a disk, simply slide the tab back over the opening.

When a disk is locked, you can't save, erase, delete, move, duplicate, or edit information on the disk. You can, however, copy files from the disk to your hard drive.

Copying and Erasing Disks

To illustrate how to copy the contents of one floppy disk to another, let's assume you have an original disk named **Master Plans**, and a blank disk named **Untitled**. To make a copy of the **Master Plans** disk, do the following:

1. Insert the **Untitled** disk in the disk drive. When its icon appears on the Desktop, press ⌘-**E** to eject it, leaving its dimmed icon on the Desktop.

2. Insert the **Master Plans** disk. When its icon appears on the Desktop, drag the icon onto the dimmed icon of **Untitled**. You know you're on target when the dimmed icon highlights.

3. Release the mouse button to start the copy process. The Mac reads the information on the **Master Plans** disk, ejects it, and prompts you to insert the disk **Untitled**. A status bar appears at the top of the screen as the copy process proceeds.

4. Insert the disks as prompted until the copy process is complete.

In this lesson, you learned about the various floppy disk types, how to initialize a disk, and how to copy a floppy disk. In the next lesson you'll learn about the printers you can use with a Mac.

Lesson 11
Macintosh Printers

In this lesson, you'll learn about the various printers available for your Macintosh, and how to connect them.

ImageWriters

The ImageWriter was Apple's first printer. It was made especially for the Mac, and uses *dot matrix* technology to produce an image on the paper. Small metal pins strike the ribbon to make dots on the paper; proper grouping of the dots makes the letters and graphics of your document. Dot matrix printers produce relatively low-quality images, but offer a trade-off in price. The current Apple ImageWriter II sells for about $600.

You can use normal 8 1/2-by-11-inch paper in an ImageWriter, or use computer paper with a perforated border (known as *continuous feed* because the sheets are connected). Typewriter-like ribbons supply the ink for the printed image. ImageWriter ribbons are inexpensive, and last for several hundred pages of printing. You can even get color ribbons for your ImageWriter.

The ImageWriter prints only what it sees on the Macintosh screen. So if your text or graphics look bad on the screen, they'll look bad when printed on an ImageWriter.

Laser Printers

Laser printers offer high-quality results for both text and graphics. If you want to create professional-quality documents, you should choose a laser printer. Listed below are features and considerations that apply to laser printers:

- Laser printers range in price from $1000 to over $10,000 (depending on features, speed, and print quality).

- Toner cartridges supply the ink. Cartridges range in price from $50 to $90 and will print about 3500 pages.

- You can use standard 8 1/2-by-11-inch paper in a laser printer, and some companies offer paper trays to accommodate 11-by-17-inch paper.

- Most laser printers are capable of printing envelopes, labels, and transparencies. Be sure, however, to buy labels that are Laser Printer approved—otherwise you may gum up the inner workings of your printer.

- Laser printers have a set of built-in fonts. These are fonts that the printer "knows" how to make. If you want to print a font that is not one of these, you will have to *download* it (transfer a copy of it) from your Mac.

StyleWriter

The StyleWriter is Apple's new low-cost alternative to a laser printer. It uses *ink-jet* technology (tiny jets shooting ink directly onto the paper) to print an image. Ink-jet printers offer a quality somewhere between that of dot matrix and laser printers. The StyleWriter sells for around $600.

At half a page per minute, the StyleWriter is relatively slow compared to a laser printers. (Most laser printers print at least 4 pages per minute.) But if speed is not a concern, the StyleWriter is an excellent value.

The StyleWriter comes with all the necessary cables, and a sheet feeder that automatically feeds up 50 sheets of paper. It can also print envelopes, labels, and transparencies.

Connecting Your Printer to Your Mac

Most Apple printers come with the necessary cables to connect them to your Mac, but you should check with your Apple dealer to make sure you have the proper cables for your printer.

The ImageWriter comes with a two cables: one for power, and one to connect it to your Mac (this one is known as a *data cable* because it carries the printing data from the Mac to the printer). Figure 11-1 shows the ImageWriter data cable.

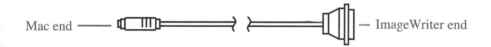

Mac end — ImageWriter end

Figure 11-1. The ImageWriter data cable.

Follow these steps to connect an ImageWriter to your Mac:

67

1. Connect the larger end of the data cable to the port on the back of the ImageWriter. The port on the ImageWriter is shaped like an elongated **D**, allowing the data cable connector to fit only one way. Once the cable is snug in the ImageWriter port, tighten down the thumbscrews on the data cable connector.

2. Plug the other end of the data cable into the printer port on the back of the Mac. It's labeled with an icon of a printer. Refer to Lesson 1 to locate the port.

3. Complete the setup by connecting the power cord from the ImageWriter to a grounded power outlet.

Connecting a LaserWriter or StyleWriter

LaserWriters use an AppleTalk cable kit to talk to the Mac. Figure 11-2 shows the components of the AppleTalk cable kit.

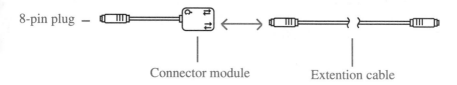

Figure 11-2. The AppleTalk cable kit.

You will need two AppleTalk kits to complete the connection of your LaserWriter. Follow the steps below to connect a LaserWriter to your Mac.

1. Insert the smaller end of one AppleTalk cable into the port on the LaserWriter. The port is labeled with an icon showing two opposite-facing arrows (this is the AppleTalk icon).

2. Insert the other AppleTalk cable into the printer port on the back of the Mac (marked with a printer icon).

3. Connect the two AppleTalk cables together, using the AppleTalk extension cable. (It has two small ends, each marked with the AppleTalk icon.)

4. Connect the power cord.

After you have physically connected your printer to your Mac, you'll need to use the Chooser DA to tell your Mac which printer you've connected. The next lesson details this operation.

Lesson 12
Printing Your Documents

In this lesson, you'll learn how to print your text documents and graphic images.

Using the Chooser to Select a Printer

Before you print, you need to tell your Mac where your printer is. You do this through the Chooser Desk Accessory (Lesson 13 explains more about additional Desk Accessories.) If your Mac is connected to a network, you may have several printers that you could print to. The Chooser enables you to select one.

Once you pick a printer using the Chooser, you do not have to change the settings again unless you want to choose a different printer. The system remembers the settings, even when you turn your Mac off.

To select a printer using the Chooser, follow these steps:

1. Make sure your printer is connected and turned on. If you have an ImageWriter, the Select light should be on. If it's not, turn it on by pressing the button under the light.

2. Drag down the **Apple** menu and select **Chooser**. The Chooser dialog box appears on the screen. Figure 12-1 shows the Chooser dialog box.

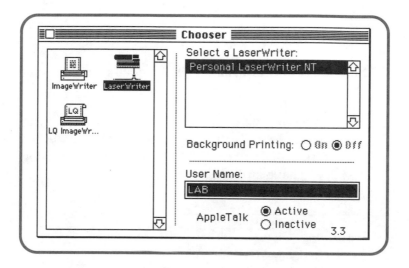

Figure 12-1. The Chooser dialog box.

3. Point and click on the icon which represents your printer, on the left side of the dialog box. The icon will highlight, and your printer's name will appear in the box to the right (labeled **Select a LaserWriter:**). If you have an ImageWriter connected directly to your Mac (not through a network), a box labeled **Select a printer port:** will show two icons: one for the printer port, and one for the modem port. Choose the port that you used to connect your printer to your Mac.

4. Select the name of your printer, and close the Chooser dialog box by clicking on the Close box in the upper left corner. You are now ready to print.

Printing Your Documents

Once you have selected a printer with the Chooser, you can print your documents and graphic images.

Use the following steps to print your documents:

1. Start the application, and open the document you want to print.

2. Drag down the `File` menu and choose `Print`. The Print dialog box appears on the screen. Figure 12-2 shows the LaserWriter dialog box. You'll see a different dialog box if you have an ImageWriter.

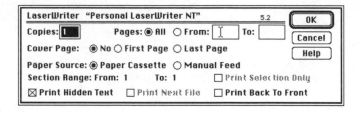

Figure 12-2. The Print dialog box.

4. Click on the `Copies` text field and enter the number of copies you want printed.

5. Select the `All` radio button to print all of the pages of your document, or enter a range in the `From:`/`To:` fields to print specific pages.

6. Click on the `OK` button. A status box appears (Figure 12-3), telling you that your document is printing. The printer will begin to print your document.

> **Printing "12 Lesson 12 (printing)"**
>
> **To cancel, hold down the ⌘ key and type a period (.).**

Figure 12-3. The printing status box.

ImageWriter Print Options

If you have an ImageWriter, you'll see a dialog box similar to the one in Figure 12-4.

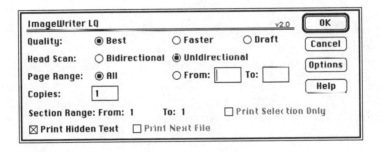

Figure 12-4. The ImageWriter Print dialog box.

The following list describes the options presented in the dialog box.

The **Quality:** option:

- **Best** offers the highest quality ImageWriter output, but at the slowest speed.

- **Faster** creates an image nearly as good as the **Best** setting, but at a slightly quicker pace.

- **Draft** prints your document in one font and type size only. This is the fastest method of printing on an ImageWriter.

The **Head Scan:** option:

- **Bidirectional** tells the ImageWriter to print while the print head is moving from left to right, AND from right to left. Bidirectional printing is slightly faster.

- **Unidirectional** prints only while the print head is moving from left to right.

The Page Setup Dialog Box

If you want to print on paper of a different size, or change the orientation of your printed page, the **Page Setup** option under the **File** menu gives you several options. Figure 12-5 shows a typical Page Setup dialog box.

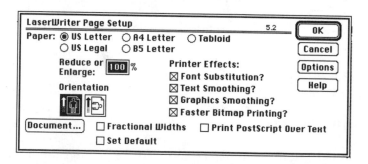

Figure 12-5. The Page Setup dialog box for a LaserWriter.

The main fields in the Page Setup dialog box you should consider are:

- Paper: Choose one of the five paper sizes. US Letter is standard 8 1/2-by-11-inch paper.

- Reduce or Enlarge: This field allows you to scale the document you print by the percentage you enter in the field. For example, enter 50% to print the image at half its original size. The default percentage is 100% (in other words, no change in the size of the printed image).

- Orientation: Select one of these two buttons to print your document in either *portrait* orientation (page taller than it is wide) or *landscape* orientation (page wider than it is tall).

Printer Change If you connect your Mac to a different printer—changing, say, from an ImageWriter to a LaserWiter—the options in the Page Setup dialog box will be different. Be sure to check the Page Setup option after switching printers.

Canceling a Print Job You can cancel the printing operation by holding down the ⌘ key and pressing the period (⌘-.); the printing will stop and the printing status box will disappear, returning you to your application.

In this lesson, you learned how to tell the Mac which printer you have, and how to print your documents. In the next lesson you'll learn about Macintosh Desk Accessories.

Desk Accessories and the Apple Menu

In this lesson, you will learn about Macintosh Desk Accessories and the Apple menu.

What is a Desk Accessory?

Desk Accessories (or *DAs*, pronounced "dee-AYS") are located in the *Apple menu*. The Apple menu, represented by the small Apple icon in the upper left corner of the menu bar, is available at all times. Consequently, you can open DAs at any time, whether you are in an application, or just working on the Desktop.

To access the DAs, pull down the Apple menu in the upper left corner of the Desktop, and choose the name of the DA you want to open. The DA will appear on the screen, and remain there until you click its Close box to put it away.

Using the Alarm Clock DA

The *Alarm Clock* displays a small box with the current time. Your Mac keeps the time and date, even when it's turned off (a small battery preserves the time and date).

Choose **Alarm Clock** from the Apple menu, and a small *clock bar* will appear, showing the current time in hours, minutes, and seconds.

You can open the clock by clicking on the small lever on the right of the clock bar. The lever will rotate down, and the clock bar will expand into a three-panel display, showing the alarm time and three additional icons: one for clock settings, one for alarm settings, and one for date settings. Figure 13-1 shows the expanded alarm clock display.

Figure 13-1. The expanded Alarm Clock.

To close the expanded display, click on the lever again. Click on the Close box to put the Alarm clock away.

Setting the Alarm

To set the alarm, follow these steps:

1. With the Alarm Clock opened into the expanded display, click on the Alarm Clock icon. The center panel will display the current alarm setting.

2. Change the alarm time by clicking on the hours digit first. The digit will highlight, and a pair of small arrows will appear to the right of the alarm time. Clicking on the Up arrow increases the hour, and clicking on the Down arrow reduces the hour. Set minutes and seconds the same way.

3. Set the alarm by clicking on the small on/off switch on the right of the alarm time panel. Close the expanded Alarm Clock back into its compact form by clicking on the lever.

The alarm will sound at the time you set—either with the system's warning beep, or with a flashing menu—depending on the **sound** setting in the *Control Panel* DA. (Lesson 18 details the Control Panel DA.)

Once the alarm goes off, the Apple menu will flash until you open the alarm clock into its expanded form, and switch it off.

Using the Calculator

The *Calculator* DA looks and operates like an ordinary desktop calculator. You can add, subtract, multiply, and divide. You can enter numbers with the keyboard, or use the mouse to point and click on the number keys on the calculator. As you type, the numbers appear on the digital display at the top of the calculator. Figure 13-2 shows the Calculator DA.

Figure 13-2. The Calculator DA.

Note Pad

The *Note Pad* gives you a place to type text notes. Figure 13-3 shows the Note Pad.

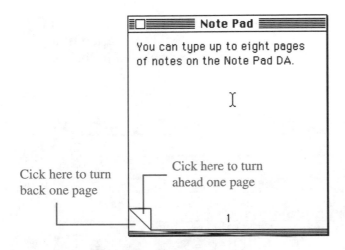

Figure 13-3. The Note Pad DA.

All the typing and editing features of the Mac operate in the Note Pad. It has eight pages available; click on the upturned corner of the note page to turn the page forward, and click below the upturned corner to flip one page back.

Key Caps

Use the *Key Caps* DA to hclp you find special characters in fonts. In most fonts you can get special characters by holding the **Option** key while typing on the keyboard. For example, hold down the **Option** and **Shift** keys and type the letter **K** (**Option-Shift-K**) to produce the character. You can find these key combinations by experimenting, but the Key Caps DA helps you locate them quickly. That's its job.

To find the special characters in a font, follow these steps:

1. Open Key Caps from the Apple menu. A new menu item called Key Caps will appear on the right of the menu bar, and the Apple keyboard will be displayed in the Key Caps window (Figure 13-4).

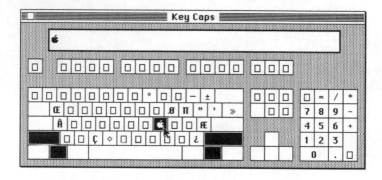

Figure 13-4. The Key Caps DA.

2. Pull down the Key Caps menu, and select from the list of fonts installed on your system. The characters of that font will appear on the keys of the keyboard.

3. Press any combination of **Shift**, **Option**, and ⌘ to see the various hidden characters of the font appear on the keyboard.

4. Once you have located the keyboard combination that types the special character you want, make a note of the key strokes (for example, **Option-Shift-K**). You can now return to your application, type the keystrokes, and the special character will appear.

Scrapbook

The *Scrapbook* DA is a holding place for text and images. You can cut, copy, and paste text and images between the Scrapbook and your documents. Figure 13-5 shows the Scrapbook window.

Current
item

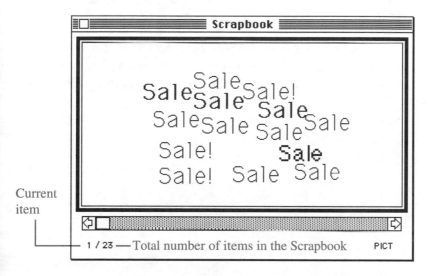

Figure 13-5. The Scrapbook DA.

The Scrapbook can hold several images. Scroll through them, using the scroll bar at the bottom of the window. The numbers in the bottom left of the window tell you how many images are in the Scrapbook (the bottom number), and which image is showing (the top number). The text in the bottom right tells you what type of image is showing, either graphic (**PICT**) or text.

To add an image to the Scrapbook, follow these steps:

1. Select the text or object you want to place in the Scrapbook.

81

2. Choose Cut or Copy from the Edit menu. The selected object will be placed on the invisible Clipboard.

3. Open the Scrapbook by dragging down the Apple menu and choosing the Scrapbook option. The Scrapbook will appear on your screen.

4. Choose Paste from the Edit menu to place the text or graphic in the Scrapbook.

In this lesson you learned about Macintosh Desk Accessories. In the next lesson, you'll find out about Macintosh applications, such as word processors and painting programs.

Lesson 14
Macintosh Applications

In this lesson you'll learn about the various Macintosh software applications available.

Software applications (or programs) are the tools you use to accomplish tasks such as writing letters and memos, analyzing a budget, or designing an organizational chart. On the less serious side, there are programs such as games, greeting card generators, and language tutors to entertain you.

Software on the Mac is easy to use because you do not have to spend time learning cryptic keystrokes each time you buy a new program. As with the consistent way you cut and paste in various Desktop operations, Mac software is highly consistent. If you learn how to draw a circle in one painting program, you do not have to relearn a different set of operations to draw a circle on another painting program.

This lesson touches on only a small part of the available software for the Mac. To learn more about Mac software, read magazines such as *MacUser* or *MacWorld*, or attend a Mac users group to talk with fellow Mac enthusiasts.

Word Processors

Word processing programs (also known as *word proces-sors*) simplify writing and editing; they allow you to type text into the computer, easily modify words and phrases as you type, and print your documents. You can revise your documents often—and print a final, corrected copy only once.

Many word processing programs offer advanced features such as footnotes, tables of contents, and outlining features, as well as spelling checkers, grammar checkers, and thesauruses that offer you an instant choice of words.

In addition to standard typing and editing features, Macintosh word processors give you precise control over the way your text appears on the screen—and thus on the printed page. Mac word processors (and all Mac software, for that matter) use an approach known as "What You See Is What You Get"—or WYSIWYG (sometimes pronounced "wizzy-wig"). If, for example, you create a document with large flowery headlines, multiple columns of text, and text flowing around pictures, you see exactly those elements on the screen. When you print the document, it will look like the screen image, only crisper. Figure 14-1 shows a typical word processing application.

Painting and Drawing Programs

Since its Desktop is a *graphical interface* (you control the computer with icons and other graphic images), the Mac excels in graphics applications. Painting and drawing programs allow you to create and edit pictures, charts, and diagrams with the same control and speed you would have in a word processor.

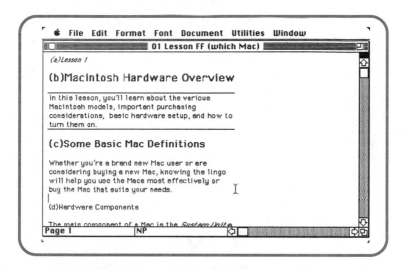

Figure 14-1. Microsoft Word screen shot.

There are two main categories of Mac graphics applications: *paint programs* and *draw programs*.

Paint programs allow you to create pictures by turning on and off individual dots of the screen, to create a *bit map* image. A bit map records the location of each dot on the screen, and whether it is turned on or off.

Consider a bit-mapped line. It is made up of several dots placed close together, end-to-end. You can turn one dot on or off without affecting other parts of the line. To change the shape or length of the line, add or delete dots until you arrive at the new shape.

Unlike paint programs, *draw programs* (or object-oriented graphic programs) allow you to create each line or object as a whole unit. To change the length of a line in a draw program, you "grab" one end and drag it to a new location. As you drag, the line stretches to meet the end-point. A mathematical description defines where the line starts and stops; when you change the image, you are changing the mathematical description—which is what the Mac remembers, instead of the location of each dot in the line.

Both paint and draw programs offer a set of tools, to draw lines and circles, and create special effects (such as airbrushing). Select a tool by clicking on its icon in a *tool palette*.

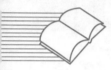

Palette A Macintosh palette is quite similar to a painter's palette. The painter uses a palette to hold and mix paints. A Mac palette holds the tools and patterns or colors you use when you paint or draw.

Figure 14-2 shows a typical drawing program, with its tool palette and some sample images.

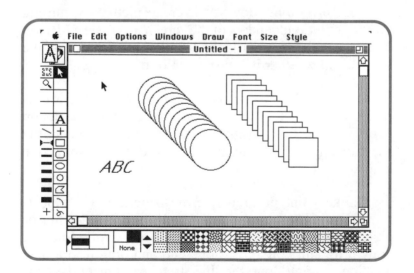

Figure 14-2. A typical drawing program.

In addition to painting and drawing tools, many programs offer *color palettes* that allow you to choose among thousands of colors (or millions, depending on your monitor).

Spreadsheets

Spreadsheets are electronic ledgers, which allow you to enter columns and rows of numbers, enter formulas to perform calculations on the numbers, and generate printouts of your work. Figure 14-3 shows a typical spreadsheet program.

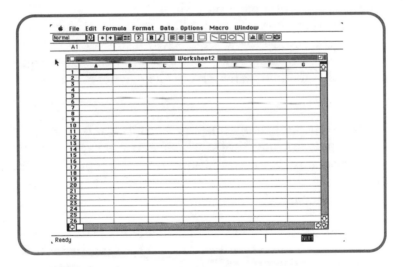

Figure 14-3. Microsoft Excel screen shot.

The true strength of a spreadsheet is its ability to perform repeated calculations and what-if calculations. You can enter a formula to add an entire column of numbers, and the next time you change any of the numbers in the column, the formula will automatically recalculate the result of your change.

Spreadsheets also offer elaborate charting and graphing features which allow you to add (for example) a pie chart to a financial planning report.

Desktop Publishing

Desktop publishing (or *DTP*) is the process of combining— in one document—text from your word processor, pictures from paint or draw programs, and charts, data, and graphs from spreadsheets.

Traditional page layout (or paste-up) is the process of physically pasting the text, pictures, fancy borders, and other elements of a page on a single sheet of paper. DTP programs such as PageMaker allow you to combine these elements on your Mac's screen. As with any Mac program, you can edit and change these parts electronically, to design documents such as sales flyers, newsletters, and even books.

Desktop publishing programs offer a robust set of menus, palettes, and tools, which allow you to control where and how the text and graphics will appear on the page. Figure 14-4 shows an Aldus PageMaker document and the tool palette.

In this lesson you learned about the mainstream software applications that are available for the Mac. In the next lesson, you'll learn how to use the basic features of these programs.

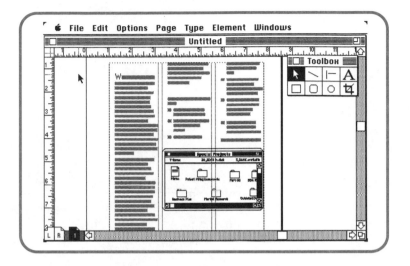

Figure 14-4. Aldus PageMaker screen shot.

Using Mac Applications

In this lesson, you'll learn to run applications, create and save new documents, and quit applications.

Application Files and Document Files

Application files contain the actual program code that carries out the operations of the program (word processing, for example). *Document files*, on the other hand, are what the application file creates. They are your letters, drawings, spreadsheets, and newsletters.

Both application files and document files have icons that represent them. Refer to Lesson 2, "The Desktop," to review the various Mac icons.

Running Applications

There are two ways to run Mac applications:

- Double-click on the application icon.

- Double-click on the document icon. If the application that created the document is on your Mac, the document will start the application.

When the application runs, it will probably display an initial screen with the manufacturer's logo, application name, and perhaps copyright information. When you arrive at the application, you will see the usual menu bar at the top of the screen, but with a few titles added.

Busy Signal If you double-click a document icon, and receive a warning telling you that the application is busy (or can't be found), don't panic. Try running an application similar to the one that created the document (another word processor, for example) and open the document with the **Open** command.

Creating New Application Documents

To start work in an application such as a word processor or painting program, you need to start a new document file. Follow the steps below to create a new *application document:*

1. Start the application by double-clicking on its icon. The application will start and present you with a blank screen, or an empty document named **Untitled**. If you get an Untitled document, you can start your work and change the document name with the **Save As...** menu choice (as detailed below).

2. If you are presented with a blank screen (no document named **Untitled**), drag down the **File** menu and choose

91

New. The application will create a new document named Untitled. Figure 15-1 shows an empty word processing document window.

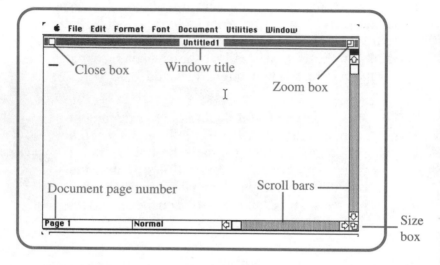

Figure 15-1. An empty document window.

The document window has all the standard window features—including the Close box, window title, Zoom box, scroll bars, and Size box. It also has a few other features, such as the page number (in the lower left corner), and the ruler (at the top of the window). Once you have the document window created, you can start work on your task at hand.

Opening Existing Application Documents

If you want to work on a document you previously created, open the document using the Open command. Follow these steps to open a existing document file:

1. Drag down the File menu and choose Open. A dialog box will appear, asking you to select a document. Figure 15-2 shows the Open dialog box for a word processor.

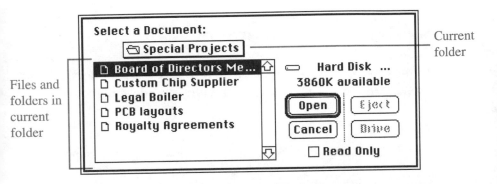

Current folder

Files and folders in current folder

Figure 15-2. The Open dialog box.

2. In the dialog box you will see a pop-up menu showing the current folder and a list of the files and folders in the current folder. If the folder has several files, the scroll bar to the right allows you to scroll through the list.

3. Click on the file name you want. The file name will highlight.

4. Click on the Open button, or press return. The dialog box will disappear and the document will open.

Quick Open To open a file quickly, you can double-click on a file name in the file name list of the Open dialog box.

If the document you are looking for is not in the current folder, point to the pop-up box containing the current folder (or disk name), then press and hold the mouse button. The box will open, and list any parent folders that exist. Drag down the list of folders, and choose a different folder. When you release the mouse button, the list of documents in the new folder will appear in the files list.

Saving Your Documents

In most programs, there are two options for saving documents: Saue and Saue As..., both under the File menu.

Save

Saue immediately saves the file under the name that is shown in the title bar of the document window. To save your document, follow these steps:

1. Drag down the File menu and choose Saue, or press ⌘-S from the keyboard. The disk drive will spin, and the mouse pointer will change to a wristwatch to indicate a short wait.

2. When the saue operation is complete, the wristwatch changes back to the mouse pointer.

Save As...

Saue As... gives you the opportunity to save the document you are working on under a name different from the one that appears in the Title Bar of the document window.

Saue As..., as the ellipsis indicates, opens a dialog box asking you for the name under which to save that file. Figure 15-3 shows a Save As... dialog box.

```
┌─────────────────────────────────────────────┐
│  ┌──────────────────────────────────────┐    │
│  │     ⬛ Master May 11th                │    │
│  ├──────────────────────────────────┬───┤    │
│  │ ▯ 01 Lesson FF (which Mac)       │▲│    │
│  │ ▯ 02 figs                        │ │    │
│  │ ▯ 02 Lesson FF (desktop l...     │▒│    │
│  │ ▯ 03 figs                        │▒│    │
│  │ ▯ 03 Lesson FF (Menus)           │▼│    │
│  ├──────────────────────────────────────┤    │
│  │ Save Current Document as:  ⬭  Hard Disk ... │
│  │ ┌──────────────────────┐   3910K available  │
│  │ │ Board Meeting Agenda │                     │
│  │ └──────────────────────┘                     │
│  │ ☐ Fast Save ☐ Make Backup  ┌──────┐ ┌─────┐ │
│  │                            │ Save │ │Eject│ │
│  │ ┌────────────┐             └──────┘ └─────┘ │
│  │ │File Format...│ Normal    ┌──────┐ ┌─────┐ │
│  │ └────────────┘             │Cancel│ │Drive│ │
│  │                            └──────┘ └─────┘ │
│  └──────────────────────────────────────────┘ │
└─────────────────────────────────────────────┘
```

Figure 15-3. A typical Save As... dialog box.

To save your document under a different name, follow these steps:

1. Drag down the File menu and choose Save As.... A dialog box will appear (see Figure 15-3).

2. Click on the file name field labeled: Save current document as: . The field will be highlighted.

3. Type a new file name of up to 32 characters.

4. Click on the OK button, or press **Return**. The mouse pointer changes to a wristwatch, and the file is saved to the disk drive.

Pick a Disk If the disk drive listed in the Save As... dialog box isn't the one you want to save the file to, click on the Drive button. The Mac will look for other disk drives, and display the contents of each one in the file list window. Note however, the Drive button will not be active unless there is a second hard drive, or a floppy disk in the floppy drive.

Closing a Document and Quitting the Program

After you have saved your work, you can quit the program, or you can close your document and create (or open) a new one, without leaving the program. To close a document, but remain in the application, do the following:

- Drag down the File menu and choose Close. If you have saved your document since you made changes to it, the document window will disappear and the applications menu bar will remain at the top of the screen.

- If you have not saved your latest changes, a warning box will appear, asking you if you want to save the document, or close the document without saving your changes, or cancel the Close operation. Choose one of these options.

Quitting

To quit an application and return to the Desktop, drag down the File menu and choose Quit, or press ⌘-Q. As before, if you have not saved your document, a warning will appear telling you so. If all your changes have been saved, the application will close the document window, and return you the Desktop.

In this lesson you learned how to run applications, and how to open and save documents. In the next lesson you'll learn about Apple's special application, HyperCard.

Understanding HyperCard

In this lesson, you'll learn about Apple's HyperCard application.

What is HyperCard?

HyperCard is like an "information Erector set." It allows you to easily build programs (called *stacks* in HyperCard) out of pre-made program parts. These parts may be text fields, windows, graphics, buttons, sounds, or animations. You can combine all of these elements into what might be called a "living" document.

Imagine the page of an encyclopedia showing a picture of the human heart, and several text passages describing its operation. The encyclopedia page is static. You either read the text, or examine the picture. If you encounter a word you don't know (such as "ventricle"), you must turn to a dictionary for a definition. And, as the text describes the flow of blood through the heart, you have to imagine the process. Nothing moves in the picture.

Now, let's recreate this presentation of information in HyperCard. The HyperCard screen would show the same picture, and the same text information. This time, however, when you encounter it/**Uentricle**, you click on it with the mouse pointer; a window appears, offering a definition and detailed picture of a ventricle.

You can read the description of blood flow (as you did on the static encyclopedia page), but you notice a button on the screen labeled it/Automate Blood Flow. You click the button, and the picture of the heart comes alive. Animated graphics show the heart pumping, valves opening and closing, and blood flowing through the heart. All the while you hear the sound of a heartbeat coming form the Mac's speaker. Keep in mind that someone has to program all this action, but HyperCard gives you the tools to organize and present information in almost any form.

Cards, Stacks, Buttons, and Fields

The HyperCard environment is made up of several elements: *stacks*, *cards*, *buttons*, *tools*, and *fields*. These elements are defined as follows:

> *Cards.* Information appears on cards. Cards can have text, pictures, buttons, and can be different sizes. Cards can be drawn to resemble common objects (such as a Rolodex card, appointment calendar, or fancy picture frame), or anything else you want. There are many pre-made cards that come with HyperCard, or you can draw your own using the painting tools available in Hyper-Card. Figure 16-1 shows several HyperCard cards.

> *Stacks.* A HyperCard stack is a collection of similar cards. Cards in stacks usually have the same appearance (a Rolodex, for example); the cards in a stack are arranged sequentially, like the pages of a book. You can move from one card to the next, in order, or skip from one to another to explore a trail of information.

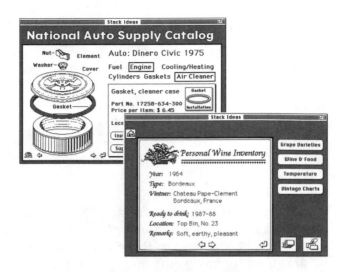

Figure 16-1. Sample HyperCard cards.

Buttons. HyperCard buttons, like the buttons in dialog boxes, start an action such as playing a sound or moving to the next card in a stack. You can create your own buttons, or use pre-made buttons. You can attach commands to buttons. The commands, known as *scripts*, tell the computer what to do when the button is pressed. For example, you could have a button that displayed the third card in a stack. Buttons can be any shape or size (Figure 16-2), and can even be invisible. For example, you could place an invisible button shaped like the outline of a country over a graphic of a map; clicking on a country would then open a card that describes the country.

Fields. HyperCard fields, like other fields in Mac programs, contain text information (such as names, addresses, or phone numbers). You can edit the information contained in a field the same way you edit any other text on the Mac.

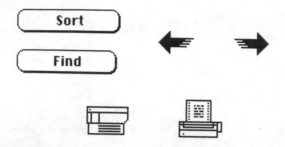

Figure 16-2. Sample HyperCard buttons.

Tools. HyperCard provides a full set of tools to help you build stacks. There is a *Button tool* that lets you draw, move, and edit buttons. The *Browse tool* (shaped like a hand) is used for navigating through cards and stacks. A full set of *Painting tools* allows you add graphics to the cards in a stack. Figure 16-3 shows the HyperCard tool palette.

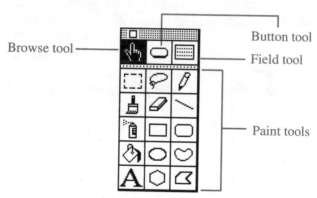

Figure 16-3. The HyperCard tool palette.

Starting HyperCard

To start HyperCard, follow these steps:

1. Turn on your computer, and open the HyperCard folder.

2. Double-click on the HyperCard icon to start the program. You will see HyperCard's opening card, the Home Card (Figure 16-4). The *Home Card* is the first card of the *Home Stack* (HyperCard's base of operation).

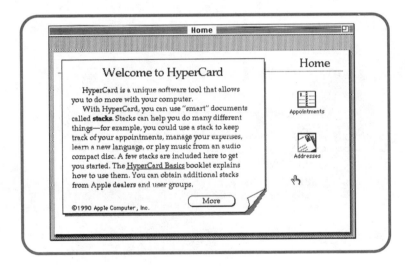

Figure 16-4. The Home Card.

The Home Stack

The Home Stack provides a place for you to access your most important stacks. There are two icons on the Home Card that represent two HyperCard stacks that came with

101

your Mac: it/Appointments and it/Addresses. You can click once on these icons (which also work as buttons) to start these stacks. As you create new stacks, you can add your own buttons to the Home Card.

Browsing HyperCard Stacks

When you are in the HyperCard environment, the mouse pointer appears as a little hand with a pointing index finger. This is known as the *Browse tool* (Figure 16-5).

Figure 16-5. The Browse tool.

You use the Browse tool to click on the buttons which appear on the cards in a stack. The result of clicking on a button depends on the button's script. Some buttons will take you from card to card, and others may take you to a different stack.

Browsing the Address Stack

Follow the steps below to browse the Addresses stack which comes with the latest version of HyperCard (2.0).

1. Start HyperCard by double-clicking on its icon. The Home Stack appears.

2. Click once on the Addresses button. The first card of the Addresses stack appears (see Figure 16-6). The card shows fields for name, address, and telephone number. You can edit the information in these fields, or create a new card and enter a new name and address.

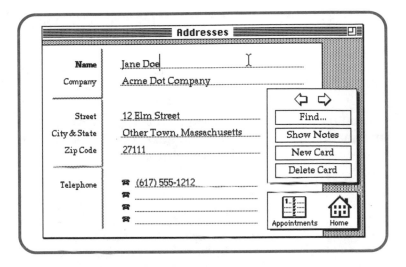

Figure 16-6. The first card of the Addresses stack.

3. Click on the right-facing arrow to move to the next card in the stack. In almost all HyperCard stacks, the right-facing arrow button moves you to the next card in the stack. The left-facing arrow moves you back one card in the stack.

4. Three other buttons under the right and left arrows allow you to find a particular name in the address stack (Find...), show a page of notes associated with this address entry (Show Notes), create a new card (New Card), or remove the current card form the stack (Delete Card). Click these buttons to explore these operations.

5. The button on the bottom right allows you to move to another stack called Appointments. The Appointments stack is similar to the Addresses stack. Use the Browse tool to explore the Appointments stack.

6. Click on the icon of a house (a typical Home button) to return to the Home card.

7. Quit HyperCard by dragging down the File menu and selecting Quit HyperCard.

In this chapter, you learned about Apple's HyperCard information environment. In the next lesson, you'll learn how to add fonts and Desk Accessories to your Mac.

Lesson 17
The Font/DA Mover Utility

In this lesson, you'll learn how to use the Font/DA Mover utility.

What Is the Font/DA Mover?

The Font/DA Mover is a program that allows you to add or remove fonts and desk accessories (DAs) from your computer.

The list of desk accessories is on the Apple (🍎) menu; you can add other desk accessories, or remove them as you wish.

The list you see in the **Font** menu shows the fonts that have been added to the System file with the Font/DA Mover.

Fonts and Desk Accessories are stored in three kinds of files: System files, special font files, and desk accessory files. Figure 17-1 shows the icons of these three file types.

Moving Fonts and DAs in System 7 System 7 eliminates the need for the Font/DA Mover. System 7 fonts and DAs have icons associated with each font or DA; you simply drag the icon into (or out of) the System Folder.

105

Fonts   Desk Accessories   System

Figure 17-1. Font and Desk Accessory file icons.

Turn off MultiFinder! The Font/DA Mover will not work properly if you have MultiFinder running. To turn off MultiFinder, Choose **Set Startup** form the **Special** menu. Click the **Finder** button. A dialog box appears, telling you that you must restart your Mac for the changes to take effect. Click **OK**, and choose **Restart** form the **Special** menu. The Mac will restart, under the control of the Finder.

Starting the Font/DA Mover Application

1. Start the Font/DA Mover program by double-clicking on its icon (Figure 17-2).

Font/DA Mover

Figure 17-2. The Font/DA Mover application icon.

Or, double-click on a Font or DA file icon. The Font/DA Mover dialog box will appear (see Figure 17-3).

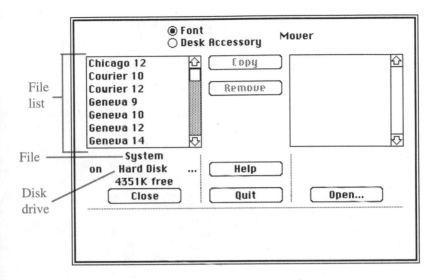

Figure 17-3. The Font/DA Mover dialog box.

If you double-click on a Font file icon, the list on the left will show the fonts contained in that file. If you chose a DA file icon, the Desk Accessories stored in the file will appear in the list.

The two buttons at the top of the dialog box allow you to work with either Fonts or DAs.

You can move fonts and DAs from one file to another. Two scrollable windows in the dialog box display the contents of the files to which (and from which) you'll be moving fonts and DAs.

Under each list of files is the name of the file you're working on (either a System, font, or DA file), and the disk it's on.

There are four buttons in the center of the dialog box: **Copy**, **Remove**, **Help**, and **Quit**.

- Click on the Copy button to copy files, either from the list on the left to the one on the right, or vice versa. You control the direction of the copy by selecting files in one list or the other.

- Click on the Remove button to delete files you selected in one list or the other.

- Click on the Help button to display the Font/DA Mover Help window. This window explains the various features of the Font/DA Mover, and how to use them.

- The Quit button allows you to leave the Font/DA Mover application.

Adding Fonts to Your System File

1. Start the Font/DA Mover by double-clicking on its icon. The Font/DA Mover dialog box appears. The list of files on the left shows the fonts in the current startup System file.

2. Click on the Open button on the right side of the dialog box. A dialog box appears; its directory shows folders and files (System, Font, and/or Desk Accessory) on the current disk, or in the current folder (Figure 17-4).

3. If the System, Font, or DA file you're looking for is not displayed in the list, you can find it by navigating through the file hierarchy. Move down by double-clicking on folder names in the file list; move up by popping open the pop-up menu at the top of the dialog box, and selecting a folder higher up the directory tree. If the file you are looking for is on a floppy disk that isn't in the drive, use the Eject button to eject the one in the drive. You can also change between disk drives by clicking on the Drive button.

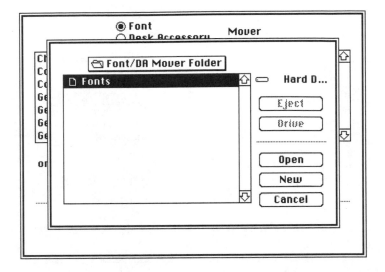

Figure 17-4. The dialog box for locating System, font, and DA files.

4. Once you have located your System, Font, or DA file, select it from the list, and click on the `Open` button (or double-click on the file name). The dialog box will disappear; the list of fonts or DAs in that file will appear in the window on the right (Figure 17-5).

5. Select the fonts or DAs you want to copy to the System file. The font or DA names will highlight, and the `Copy` button will become active with arrows pointing left (Figure 17-5). Notice also that a sample of the font you selected appears at the button of the dialog box.

6. Click on the `Copy` button. The Font/DA Mover begins to copy the files to the System file.

7. Click on the `Quit` button to exit the Font/DA Mover application.

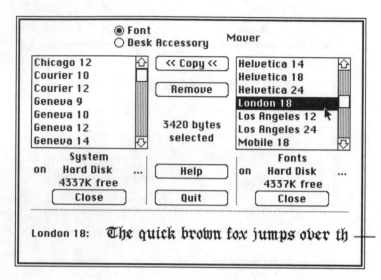

Figure 17-5. Ready to copy the London font to the System file.

In this lesson you learned how to add and remove fonts and Desk Accessories. In the next lesson, you'll learn how to customize your Mac with the Control Panel DA.

Lesson 18
Understanding the System Folder

In this lesson, you'll learn about the Mac's operating system, and special System Folder.

What is an Operating System?

An *operating system* is the program that tells your computer how to behave. It talks to the screen, displays the menus, windows, and characters, talks to the disk drives, interprets the keys you press on the keyboard, and so on.

On the Macintosh, the operating system is called the *System*. The System is a program that resides in a special folder named *System Folder*. The System Folder must be on your hard drive, or on a startup floppy disk if you don't have a hard drive. Figure 18-1 shows the System Folder icon.

System Folder

Figure 18-1. The System Folder icon.

There is second file which must be in the System Folder if your Mac is to start up properly. It's named *Finder*. You may recall (from Lesson 2) that another name for the Desktop is the Finder. The Finder is the *user interface* of your Mac. It tells the Mac how to display the menus at the top of the screen, how the Trash icon should handle trash, and so on. Figure 18-2 shows the System and Finder icons.

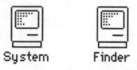

System   Finder

Figure 18-2. The System and Finder icons.

When you turn your Mac on, it looks for the System Folder on the Startup drive. The *Startup drive* (or *volume*, as a disk drive is sometimes called) is designated through the Control Panel. When you turn your Mac on, it first looks to see if there is a hard drive, and if the hard drive has a System Folder containing the proper files. If the Mac can't find the folder or files, or if there is no hard drive, it looks at the floppy drive for a disk with the files. If there are no files to be found there, the Mac displays a small disk icon with a flashing **X** in its center. If this happens, insert the disk named System Tools that came with your Mac, and your Mac should start normally.

Identifying Software Versions

Like other Mac software, the System and Finder programs are periodically updated to include new and enhanced features. Each time programs are updated, the maker of the program assigns a version number to it, to help keep track of the changes. Although you do not *have* to update your computer each time a new version of these files is released, it's a good idea to stay current. Check with your Apple dealer to find out more about the latest release of these files.

To find out what version number of the System and Finder files on your Mac, follow these steps:

1. At the Desktop (not in an application), pull down the Apple (⬢) menu and select the first menu item, About the Finder (Figure 18-3).

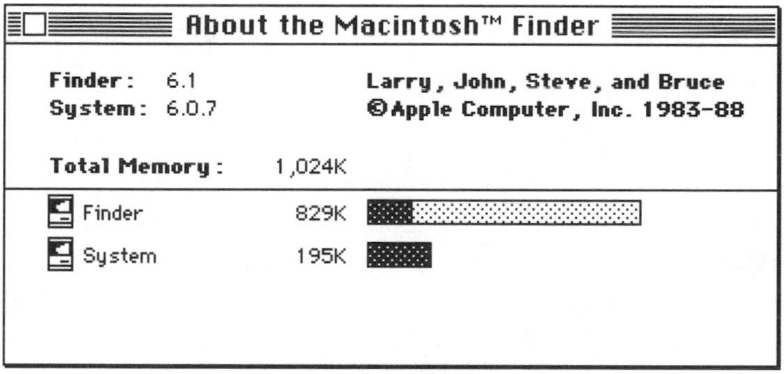

Figure 18-3. The Finder version window.

If you own a newer Mac that runs System 7, the first menu item may read About this Macintosh (Figure 18-4).

2. Locate the version numbers of the System and Finder; they should be in the top half of the dialog box. Notice also that the total amount of RAM is listed below the version numbers.

113

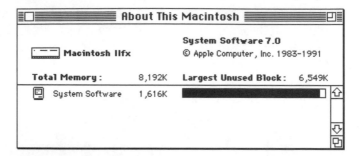

Figure 18-4. The version information window for System 7.

Other Items That Belong in the System Folder

There are other programs and files that are placed in the System Folder to enhance your Mac, or provide resources for your application software. Most software installation programs place the appropriate files in the System Folder when you install them, or give specific instructions regarding which files to drag to the System Folder. However, it doesn't hurt to know the general types of files that belong there. Here is a list of the most popular kinds of files to add to a typical System Folder:

- *Control Panel Devices* (CDEV, pronounced "SEA-dev"). These files represent the functions available in the Control Panel DA. Examples of these files include **Sound**, **Monitors**, **Color**, and **Keyboard**.

- *Initialization resources* (INITs). INITs are files that load into the Mac when you first turn it on. One example of an INIT is a virus protection program. It loads as the first program in your computer so it can check all subsequently-loaded programs for virus activity.

- *PostScript Fonts.* These files hold the description that a laser printer needs to draw the characters of a font. Your Mac automatically sends these files to the laser printer when you print a document that uses the font.

System 7

If you have purchased a new Mac, the version of the System file is probably 7. Apple calls this version "System 7." You'll learn more about System 7 in Lesson 21, "System 7 Enhancements." For now, let's explore how System 7 affects the System Folder.

System 7 reduces the complexity of the System Folder by organizing its files into sub-folders, and by making it intelligent. Files such as Control Panel Devices and INITs are automatically placed into folders named Control Panels and Extensions. When you want to add a file such as a CDEV, you don't have to decide where the file goes; the Mac knows, and takes care of it for you. You simply drag a Control Panel Device file into the System Folder icon, and the Mac automatically puts the file in the Control Panels folder. Fonts and other special system files are organized and managed in the same way.

In this lesson you learned about the Mac's operating system, and the special System Folder. In the next lesson, you'll learn how to work with the Mac Control Panel DA.

Lesson 19
Control Panel DA

In this lesson, you'll learn about the Control Panel DA.

What is the Control Panel?

The Control Panel is a Desk Accessory that lets you modify settings on your Mac such as time and date, speaker volume, mouse behavior, and the pattern and color of the Desktop. Figure 19-1 shows the Control Panel window.

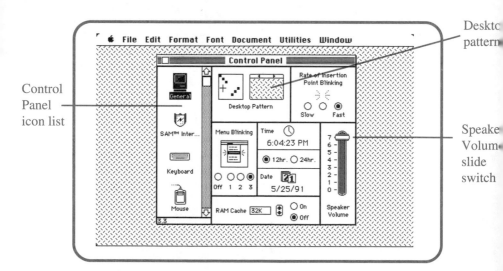

Figure 19-1. The General Control Panel.

116

Using the General Control Panel

When you choose the **Control Panel** from the **Apple** menu, you'll see a screen similar to Figure 19-1. Notice that there are several icons in a scrollable window on the left side of the panel. When you select any of these icons, features related to the icon appear at the right. In this case, the **General** icon is highlighted. Here is a closer look at some of its controls. Your Mac may display other selections as well. (Consult your Macintosh manual to find out how to use these selections.)

The cells in the **General** panel allow you to configure the following general items:

Desktop Pattern: Controls the dots in the Desktop pattern, and their color. (Using this cell is detailed below; the other cells are used in a similar way.)

Rate of Insertion Point Blinking: Controls how fast the insertion point blinks on and off.

Time and Date: Sets the time and date of the internal system clock.

Menu Blinking: Controls the speed at which the menu title blinks when you choose a keyboard shortcut to a menu command.

Speaker Volume: Controls the volume of the internal Mac speaker.

117

Changing the Desktop Pattern

To change the pattern of your Desktop, follow these steps:

1. Move the mouse pointer into the cell labeled `Desktop Pattern`. The pointer will change to a plus sign. On the right is a miniature version of the Desktop, showing the current pattern. On the left is a cell containing the dots that make up the pattern you see on the Desktop.

2. Click on an empty part of the left-hand cell to add dots to the pattern, or click on an existing dot to turn it off. If you have a color Mac, you can change the color of the dots by clicking on one of the six color blocks at the bottom of the `Desktop Pattern` cell. As you add or remove dots, the pattern on the right reflects your changes.

3. Clicking on the small Desktop replica on the right will apply the pattern to the real Desktop. The entire Desktop will change to the pattern you selected.

Using the Color Control Panel

If you have a color Mac, the Control Panel will have a color icon (shaped like an artist's palette) in the list on the left. Select this icon to change the color of highlighted text or icons. A sample of the current highlight color is shown on the right. Click on the `Change Color` button to modify the highlight color. A dialog box showing a round color wheel appears (Figure 19-2).

Use the mouse pointer to choose a new color, and click on `OK` when you are finished. The next time you select an icon, or highlight a section text, the highlight will be the color you selected.

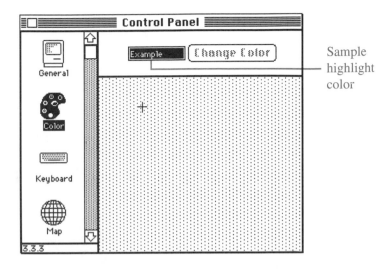

Figure 19-2. The Color Control Panel dialog box.

Using the Keyboard Control Panel

The Keyboard Control Panel (see Figure 19-3) allows you to choose the rate at which characters are typed when you press and hold a key on the keyboard.

You can also choose the amount of time you must wait before characters will repeat automatically when a key is held down. Simply click on the radio button that describes the speed and delay that you want.

Using the Mouse Control Panel

The Mouse Control Panel (see Figure 19-4) allows you to choose the speed at which the mouse tracks, and the double-click speed of the mouse button.

119

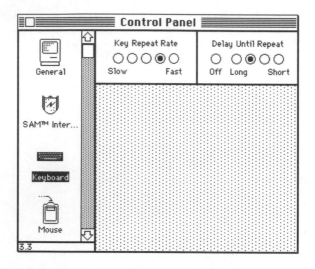

Figure 19-3. The Keyboard Control Panel.

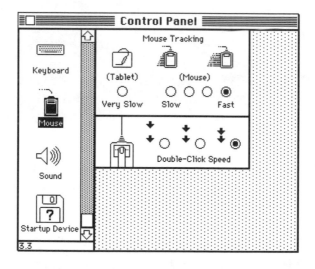

Figure 19-4. The Mouse Control Panel.

Tracking describes how fast the mouse pointer moves across the screen when you move the mouse. If you want the pointer to move a lot when you move the mouse a little, choose the **Fast** setting. If want finer control over the mouse pointer position, choose one of the settings to the left.

Double-Click Speed indicates the amount of time between each click of a double click. Select the far right radio button (downward-pointing arrows closest together) if you want to tap the mouse very quickly to produce a double click. If you want to tap out the two clicks a little slower, choose one of the left settings (arrows a little farther apart).

Using the Sound Control Panel

The Sound Control Panel (Figure 19-5) allows you to set the volume of sound on your Mac, as well as the type of alert sound you hear when you click outside a dialog box or commit some other no-no.

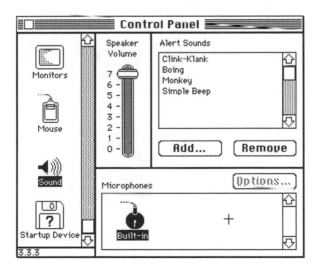

Figure 19-5. The Sound Control Panel.

Set the speaker volume by pointing to the slide switch in the Volume cell, and dragging it up or down; this increases or decreases the volume. When you release the mouse button, the warning beep will sound at the volume you select. If you set the volume slider to **0**, no sound will be played; instead, the menu bar at the top of the Desktop will flash to indicate an alert condition.

To select the type of alert sound, click on one of the sound names in the list on the right. (Most Macs come with **Boing, Clink-Clank, Monkey**, or **Simple Beep**; your list may contain more or fewer choices.) The sound you click on will play.

Adding Your Own Alert Sound

If you have a Mac II si or Mac II LC, the panel below the Alert Sound panel will show a microphone icon. To record your own Alert sound using the microphone that came with your Mac, follow the steps below.

1. Make sure the microphone is plugged into the port on the back of your Mac. The port is labeled with a small microphone icon.

2. Select the **Sound** icon in the control panel list. The sound control panel will appear on the right.

3. Click on the **Add** button. A dialog box will appear (see Figure 19-6) showing a progress meter and five buttons (**Record, Stop, Pause, Play**.)

4. Click on the **Record** button and talk into the microphone. The progress bar shows how much time you have to record (a total of about 10 seconds).

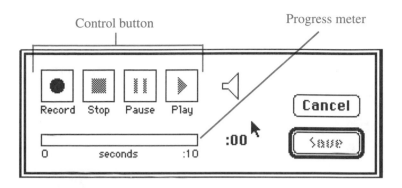

Figure 19-6. The Add Alert Sound dialog box.

5. Click on the Stop button to stop recording. You can play your message back by clicking on the Play button. Re-record the sound as many times as you wish, until you're satisfied with the result.

7. Click on the Save button. A dialog box will appear, asking you to name the sound you recorded. Name the Alert sound you created, and return to the main Control Panel by clicking on the OK button. The sound name you recorded will appear in the list of Alert sounds.

8. Select your new sound by clicking on its name.

9. Close the control panel by clicking on the Close box in the upper left corner. The next time the Mac encounters an alert condition, your sound will play.

In this lesson you learned how to customize the look and feel of your Mac using the Control Panel. In the next lesson, you'll learn how to troubleshoot common Mac problems and error messages.

Mac
Troubleshooting

In this lesson, you'll learn about Mac error messages and how to troubleshoot common Mac hardware and software problems.

With its Desktop interface and consistent menus and commands, the Mac is easy to use. But even with this simplicity, you are likely to encounter error messages, and find yourself wondering what to do next. The following Problem/ Solution format gives answers to some common Mac problem areas.

1. **Problem:** *Missing Startup.* When you start your Mac, a picture of a disk with a flashing **X** in its center appears, and the Desktop does not come up.

   Solution: When this happens, the Mac cannot find a *startup volume.* A valid startup volume is one that contains a folder named System Folder. Within the System Folder there must be a System file and a Finder File. Locate the disk labeled System Startup that came with your Mac. Insert it in the floppy drive, and the Mac should start. Make sure the hard disk contains a System Folder with the System and Finder files in it.

2. **Problem:** *Sad Mac.* An icon of a Sad Macintosh shows up when you turn your Mac on, and nothing else happens.

Solution: There is a hardware problem with your computer. You should take your Mac to an authorized Apple dealer for diagnosis and repair. All Macs come with a 1-year warranty on hardware components. Check with your dealer to see if your Mac is covered.

3. **Problem:** *Jumpy Mouse.* The mouse pointer jumps around on the screen when you move it the mouse.

   Solution: Your mouse is probably dirty. Shut down the Mac, and turn the mouse over. Pop open the plastic ring that holds the mouse ball in place, either by twisting counter-clockwise (older mice), or sliding towards the arrow on the plastic ring. Let the ball drop out, and clean it with a dry cloth. Use a cotton swab and alcohol to clean dirt from the little rollers inside the mouse. Reassemble the mouse and test its operation. If the problem continues, you may have to purchase a new mouse.

4. **Problem:** *Missing or busy application.* You double-click on a document icon to open it (as a way of starting its application), and you receive a message similar to Figure 20-1.

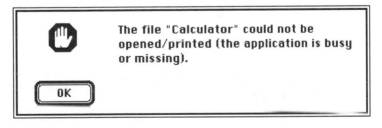

Figure 20-1. The "missing application" error message.

Solution: This message means the Mac can't find the application that created the document, or the file is a System file used by the Mac. Try opening the file by first starting a similar application, and choosing Open under the File menu. If the application recognizes the file, its name will appear in the Open dialog box. You can then double-click on the file name to open it into its window.

5. **Problem:** *Unreadable disk.* You insert a disk in the floppy disk drive, and the Mac displays the message in Figure 20-2:

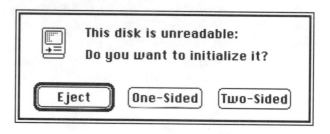

Figure 20-2. The "unreadable disk" message.

Solution: You've inserted a disk which is probably blank, not Mac-formatted (a DOS disk, for example), or formatted on a newer Mac than the one you're using (older hardware often has trouble with newer formats). If you are sure the disk is blank, and you're willing to lose any data that might be on it, click on OK to initialize it. If you suspect that the disk has Mac data on it, try inserting the disk into a newer Mac, and copying the files to an 800K (Double Density) disk. All but the oldest Macs can read 800K disks.

6. **Problem:** *Bomb!* The Mac unexpectedly displays the System Bomb! error message, and freezes the keyboard.

Solution: This is usually an indication that multiple System files are present in the computer. The Mac gets them confused, and "panics" with the System Bomb message. Try to locate all the System files on the hard disk—and throw them in the Trash, keeping only the latest version.

7. **Problem:** *Can't open printer.* The Mac displays an error message similar to the one in Figure 20-3.

Figure 20-3. The "Can't open printer" error message.

Solution: You have not told the Mac which printer you're using. Save the document you're trying to print, and open the Chooser Desk Accessory from the Apple (🍎) menu. Click on the icon that represents your printer, and follow the other instructions that appear. Then close the Chooser DA, and try to print your document again.

8. **Problem:** *Re-insert disk.* The Mac displays a message asking you to reinsert a disk you recently ejected.

Solution: When you eject a disk using the Eject command in the File menu, the Mac remembers the disk—and may ask to see it again. Also notice the dimmed icon of the disk on the Desktop. If you don't need to access the files on the disk (this same message occurs when copying files from one floppy to another), press ⌘-period to tell the Mac forget about the disk and go on. To avoid this problem in the future, you can eject disks by dragging them to the Trash; this tells the Mac to forget about the disk.

In this lesson, you learned how to respond to common Mac error messages. In the next lesson, you'll learn about System 7, and how it can make using your Mac more convenient.

Lesson 21
System 7
Enhancements

In this lesson, you'll learn about System 7, Apple's new Macintosh operating system.

What is System 7?

As you learned in Lesson 2 on the Desktop, and in Lesson 18 on the Mac System Folder, the system software of a computer controls how the computer performs tasks, and how you interact with the computer to accomplish your productivity goals. System 7 is Apple's latest version of Macintosh system software.

Throughout this book, special System 7 icons help you identify areas of operation which might be different if you are running System 7. The basic operations of the Mac, however, are the same under the control of System 7. Pulling down menus, working with icons and folders, responding to dialog boxes, and editing text all operate (for the most part) the same way they do in System 6.0.

So what's so great about System 7? The next few sections outline some of the differences you will encounter, and how System 7 can make working and playing with your Mac even easier.

A New Look to the Desktop

In System 7, the Desktop looks very much the same as it does in older system versions, with a few exceptions. Figure 21-1 shows a typical System 7 Desktop.

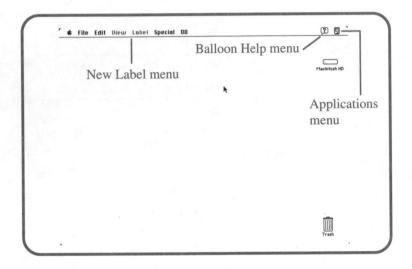

Figure 21-1. The System 7 Desktop.

Labels

Notice the new menu (**Label**) in the menu bar at the top of the screen. The **Label** menu lets you tag icons with a specific color and text label. Using the **Label** menu, you can quickly organize and identify programs, documents, and folders.

For example, you might label urgent memos with red and an "Urgent" label. When you view the files tagged with labels, the *icon view* shows only the color associated with the label. The *list views* (such as **Name** and **Date**) show text label and color (in our example, the "Urgent" label in red). For more details on icon view and list view, you might want to review Lesson 5.

To apply a label to an icon, select the icon, and drag down the label menu and choose the **Label** selection. The icon will change to the **Label** color; if the icon is in a folder viewed as a list, the text part of the label will appear to the right of the file name.

You can also customize the color and text of the labels in the **Label** menu by using the new Views Control Panel.

Balloon Help

The small icon of a cartoon balloon containing a question mark is useful for newcomers and Mac veterans alike. This is the *Balloon Help menu* (Figure 21-2).

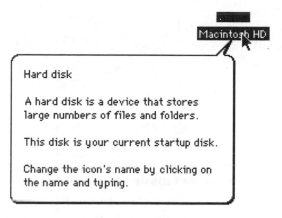

Figure 21-2. Balloon Help in action.

131

To use the Balloon Help menu, follow these steps:

1. Drag down the Balloon Help menu.

2. Choose **Show Balloons**. Now, when ever you point the mouse pointer at an icon, menu, or just about any object, a small balloon appears next to the object—containing a description of the object and how it's used.

3. You can turn Balloon Help off by pulling down the Balloon Help menu and choosing **Turn Off Balloon Help**.

Many new software applications (written with System 7 in mind) customize the Balloon help feature. You can easily learn about the various features of the application by turning on the Balloon Help, and browsing around its menus and dialog boxes.

The Application Menu

Next to the Balloon Help menu icon is an icon of a small Mac. This is the *Applications menu* (Figure 21-3.)

Figure 21-3. The Applications Menu.

In System 7, each time you open an application or Desk Accessory, its name is added to the Applications menu. Using this menu, you can switch easily from one open application to another. As long as you don't Quit the application, its name will stay on the Applications menu.

This feature replaces the MultiFinder feature used in older Mac System versions. Unlike MultiFinder, the Applications menu is always turned on. (You could elect to turn MultiFinder on or off at Startup in older Mac Systems.)

The number of applications you can have open at one time depends on the amount of RAM your Mac has installed. For most Macs, you'll need at least 3 megabytes of RAM to open more than two applications at one time.

Adding Items to the Apple Menu

Although the Apple menu appears to be the same as its earlier versions (at first), opening it reveals a new look. Each menu item has an icon to help you identify the function of the menu selection. Figure 21-4 shows the new Apple (🍎) menu.

The Chooser icon is two AppleTalk cable connectors, indicative of selecting a printer. The Alarm Clock icon is an old-fashioned alarm clock, and the Calculator icon resembles a calculator. Aside from its new look, the Apple menu has an important enhancement. In older Mac system version, you have to use the Font/DA Mover programs to add a Desk Accessory to the Apple menu. In System 7, you simply drag the DA icon to a sub-folder of the System Folder, labeled Apple Menus. The next time you open the Apple menu, the new DA appears in the list, icon and all.

Figure 21-4. The new Apple (🍎) menu under System 7.

Enhancing the Views of Your Folders and Disks

In System 7, you move and copy files and folders as usual: point, click, and drag from one location to another. You'll notice, however, that the appearance of your folders' contents has been improved significantly. Figure 21-5 shows the new list view of a System 7 folder.

The small triangles next to the folders in the list allow you to look at a folder's contents in outline form. If the triangle points down, the folder's contents are displayed; if the triangle is pointing right, the folder's contents are not displayed (that is, they are *collapsed*). In Figure 21-5, the System Folder is collapsed, and the Utilities folder is expanded.

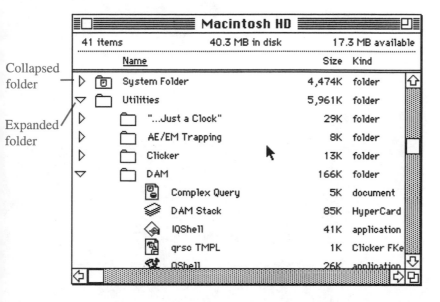

Collapsed folder

Expanded folder

Figure 21-5. The new and improved list view for folders.

Summary

In this lesson you learned about Apple's new Macintosh system software, System 7. Now that you have learned about the Mac's graphical approach to computing—by way of the Desktop, menus, windows and dialog boxes—and you've explored the available hardware additions and software applications, you've completed the *10 Minute Guide to the Mac.*

Overtime

Glossary

Active window—The window in which you are currently working. The active window is characterized by several lines in its title bar.

Alert box—A box that appears on screen to give you a reminder or a warning pertaining to your current operation.

Apple key—Also known as the Command key. See *Command key*.

Apple menu—The menu under the Apple symbol located in the top left corner of the Desktop.

AppleTalk—A set of software and hardware conventions that allow Macs to be connected together by cable, sharing files and other devices (such as printers).

Application—Software used to accomplish specific tasks, such as writing (word processors), financial calculations (spreadsheets), or drawing (graphics programs).

Bit map—An image that is made up of dots, and consequently stored in memory. The Mac screen and ImageWriter use bit map images in their output.

Bomb—A malfunction that causes your computer to stop working. The Bomb icon appears in an alert box when your Mac encounters an internal error that it can't recover from. You must restart your Mac to recover from a Bomb.

Button—A graphic representation of a control button, appearing in dialog boxes. You click on the button with the mouse pointer to initiate the action described by the button's text label.

Byte—One character of data. A byte equals 8 smaller units of measure called *bits*.

Calculator—A Mac Desk Accessory that operates like a common desktop calculator.

Cancel—Backing out of an activity. When Cancel appears as a button in a dialog box, you have the opportunity to leave the box without changing the way its options were set when you opened it.

CDEV—Control Panel Device, a program which allows you to customize your Mac's features (such as speaker volume). Activated through the Control Panel, CDEV files are stored in the *System Folder*.

Checkbox—A type of Macintosh button which has an Off state (empty) and an On state (checked with an **X**) to indicate a choice of option.

Chooser—A Desk Accessory used to choose which printer your Mac prints to. The Chooser also assists in selecting network connections.

Clicking—Pressing and releasing the button on a mouse.

Clipboard—An area of computer memory used for temporary storage of the text or images cut or copied from a document. The Clipboard is used to transfer objects between different applications.

Close box—A small box in the upper right corner of a window. Clicking on the Close box collapses the window into its icon form, or closes an application document.

Command key—A key on the Mac keyboard that is used in conjunction with other keys or mouse activities. Many keyboard shortcuts to menu commands use the Command key. Also known as the Apple key and Clover key, since the and ⌘ characters appear on the key.

Control Panel—A Desk Accessory that allows you to modify Mac features such as sound volume, speed of double-clicking, and the pattern on the Desktop.

CPU—Central Processing Unit, the microprocessor of a computer that performs the bulk of the calculations necessary for the computer to function.

DA—Desk Accessory. Small convenience programs that usually emulate common objects found on a real-life desk (such as a calculator or notepad).

Desktop—Also known as the *Finder*. This is the basic operating environment of the Macintosh, made up of the windows, icons, menus, and pointers associated with the Macintosh operating system.

Dialog box—A box on the Mac screen that contains buttons and fields. You enter information into a dialog box to add more information to a command or operation.

Document—The file you create with an application program, such as a letter in a word processing application.

Double-clicking—Pointing to an object on the screen, then tapping the mouse button twice in rapid succession. Double-clicking opens icons or runs application programs.

Dragging—Moving an object on the screen by pointing to the object with the mouse pointer, then pressing and holding the mouse button while moving the mouse.

Edit menu—A standard menu found in most applications and on the Desktop. Commands such as Cut, Copy, and Paste are in the Edit menu.

Ellipsis—The symbol (...). Ellipsis next to a menu item (e.g., Print...) indicate that a dialog box is present for that item.

Field—A boxed area within dialog boxes and other Mac applications, used to enter text information such as file names.

File menu—A standard Mac menu found in all Mac applications. File and printing functions such as Save, Open, and Print are found on this menu.

Finder—The Macintosh system file that creates and manages the Desktop, including the mouse pointer, menus, windows, and Trash Can. (The term is also used to mean the Desktop itself.)

Floppy disk—A removable magnetic storage device used to store and transport computer files.

Folder—Manila-folder-shaped icons on the Mac Desktop that help you organize your files. You can place files (and other folders) inside folders.

Font/DA Mover—A Macintosh utility program that allows you to add Fonts and Desk Accessories to your Mac, and/or remove them.

Hard disk—A non-removable magnetic storage device used to store large quantities of files. Hard disks are much faster than floppy disks, and can be either internal or external to your Mac.

Hardware—The physical components of a computer, such as the monitor, disk drives, mouse, and keyboard.

Highlighting—Also known as *selecting*, this process changes the color or reverses the black-and-white of an object on your screen (such as an icon or section of text), to indicate that the object is to receive the action of the next command you choose.

I-beam pointer—The flashing vertical bar used to show where characters will appear when you type.

Icon—A small picture that usually represents a real-life object (such as a folder or trash can). Files, commands, and applications all have icons associated with them.

INIT—A small program which is activated when you start your Mac. INITs (such as virus protection) are most often used to enhance the operation of your Mac.

Initialize—To place formatting information on a floppy or hard disk so the Mac can later place files on the disk.

K (Kilobyte)—1024 bytes. A common unit used to measure the memory capacity of computers.

Laser printer—A high-quality printer that uses a laser to tell its other components where to place ink on the paper.

M (Megabyte)—1024 kilobytes, or about a million bytes. The capacities of hard disks and high-density floppy disk drives are usually measured in megabytes.

Memory—The circuits in a computer used to store the programs you use.

Menu—A list of commands, functions, or programs available for your use.

Message box—A box that appears on the screen indicating a warning, caution, or confirmation of an action.

Modem—A device used to communicate with other computers over the telephone lines; the term stands for MOdulate-DEModulate.

Monitor—The screen of a computer.

Mouse—A hand-operated device used to direct action on the computer screen. A *mouse pointer* moves on the screen as the mouse moves on the table top.

MultiFinder—Macintosh system software that allows you to load multiple applications at one time.

Network—A group of computers connected together (usually with cables); also, a software application used to share files, printers, and other resources.

Open—To load a document file into an application program, or double-click on an icon to expand it into its window form.

Operating system—Essential software that controls the operation of a computer.

Palette—A window that contains several icons of tools (such as drawing pencil, eraser, or paintbrush).

Paste—To place the contents of the Clipboard into a document.

Pointer—The indicator on the screen that shows the movement of the mouse.

Pop-up menu—A list of available options in a dialog box. All but one of the items on the list stays hidden until you click and hold on the menu's box.

Port—A hardware connecting point on a computer, such as the keyboard cable port.

Program—Another name for application.

Quit—To leave an application. The Quit menu selection is located in the File menu in most programs.

Radio buttons—A group of round control buttons that resemble car-radio buttons. Only one of the buttons in the group can be on at one time.

RAM—Random-Access Memory. The working area of the computer used to store the information on which it is currently working. The contents of RAM are lost when the computer is turned off.

Restart—The act of turning the Mac off and then on again, without using the power on switch. The Restart menu selection is located on the Special menu.

ROM—Read-Only Memory. Chips in the Mac that contain the programs that tell the Mac how to be a Mac. ROM does not forget its contents when you power off the Mac.

Save—A menu selection in the File menu that transfers your documents from RAM to a floppy or hard disk.

Save As—A menu selection in the File menu that allows you to change the name of a document before saving it to a disk.

Scrapbook—A Desk Accessory used to store multiple objects, in both text and graphic form.

Shift-Click—A method of selecting multiple icons. Hold down the Shift key, and click on icons to select them.

Shut Down—The command that prepares the Mac to be turned off (or actually turns off newer Macs). Shut Down is found on the Special menu.

Submenu—A menu within a menu, indicated by a small triangle next to the main menu item.

System Folder—A must-have folder on the Mac, which contains the System file and Finder file.

Title bar—The top part of a window, which contains the Close box, the Zoom box, and the name of the window (this is also the name of the icon when the window is closed).

Trash—A special icon, shaped like a trash can, located on the Mac Desktop. The Trash is used to delete files from the Macintosh.

Undo—A standard Mac command which reverses the last operation you performed. Some operations (such as Save) can't be undone.

Index

145